ENGLISH 101

Guidebook & Reader

Seventh Edition

ENGLISH 101 FACULTY

Editors

Thomas Sura
Undergraduate Writing Coordinator

David Beach
Associate Undergraduate Writing Coordinator

West Virginia University
Department of English

HAYDEN McNEIL

Printed in the United States of America

10 9 8 7 6 5 4 3 2 1

ISBN 978-0-7380-7106-0

Hayden-McNeil Publishing
14903 Pilot Drive
Plymouth, MI 48170
www.hmpublishing.com

Sura 7106-0 F15

TABLE OF CONTENTS

ACKNOWLEDGMENTS

The selections written by WVU faculty and students are copyrighted by the respective authors and are published with their permission.

Thank you to the Undergraduate Writing Program Committee and the English 101 faculty at WVU for their excellent contributions. Special acknowledgments are extended to the following:

David Beach

Laura Brady

Clint Wilson

Rebecca Thomas

Yvonne Hammond

Kelly Diamond

Successful writers are not the ones who write the best sentences. They are the ones who keep writing. They are the ones who discover what is most important and strangest and most pleasurable in themselves, and keep believing in the value of their work, despite the difficulties.

—BONNIE FRIEDMAN, *WRITING PAST DARK*

SOCIAL JUSTICE

The West Virginia University community is committed to creating and fostering a positive learning and working environment based on open communication, mutual respect, and inclusion.

If you are a person with a disability and anticipate needing any type of accommodation in order to participate in this class, please advise your instructor and make appropriate arrangements with the Office of Accessibility Services (304-293-6700). For more information on West Virginia University's Diversity, Equity, and Inclusion initiatives, please see http://diversity.sandbox.wvu.edu/ddei.

PREFACE

I was in a restaurant eating lunch and watching the WVU men's basketball team on the television. While I was eating, two men sat down next to me wearing bright red Detroit Red Wings hockey jerseys.

Since I grew up in Michigan, I asked them if they were from Michigan, too. From there we started talking about sports, school, and jobs. Both of them were students.

I asked, "Do you guys write much?"

"No," they both said. "We're going to be physical therapists, and our professors don't assign papers."

What our conversation had uncovered is the single biggest misconception about writing, especially in courses like English 101. It is the idea that only "writers" write. In other words, many people think that the only reason they will ever need to write is if they become novelists, screenwriters, or journalists—jobs that have writing as a central focus.

The truth is that writing is vital to virtually every aspect of life from the professional to the personal. Sure, writing will take different forms (genres) at different times (contexts), but writing will help you no matter who you are or what you choose to do in life.

I asked my new friends if they had ever tried reading for 20 minutes and then writing for 5 minutes about what they had just read.

"No," they said. They hadn't thought about that.

I asked them if they knew that Curt Shilling, the phenomenal Major League Baseball pitcher, regularly wrote in a notebook to help him keep track of the hitters he faced so that he knew what pitches to throw to them and when.

"Really?" they replied.

Yes.

Like the conversation I've just described, this course is designed to introduce you to many of the ways you can use writing. While we will always place emphasis on communicating ideas to audiences, we will also explore other ways you can use writing including to invent new ideas, tell stories, solve problems, question arguments, and make plans. I think you will find that all of this work with writing can be relevant to you as a college student, especially as you grapple with challenges like studying for classes, choosing majors, and developing from students to professionals. It doesn't matter if you're a physical therapist, an engineer, a nurse, or even a pitcher in Major League Baseball. Writing can help you excel.

We hope you enjoy learning about writing as much as we enjoy teaching. Have a wonderful semester.

— Tom Sura

WELLWVU®
The Students' Center of Health

Health & Education Building
390 Birch Street
PO Box 6422
Morgantown, WV 26506-6422
Adjacent to the Student Rec Center

Carruth Center for Psychological & Psychiatric Services • 2nd Floor • 304-293-4431 • well.wvu.edu/ccpps
Drop-in hours: Monday-Friday, 8:15 a.m.-4:45 p.m. • Extended evening hours by appointment: Monday-Thursday

- Group, individual, and crisis counseling
- Psychiatric evaluation, consultation and medical management
- Student Assistance Program (SAP) for alcohol and drug counseling
- MindFit screening, testing and treatment for attentional and other learning difficulties
- Consultation to students, parents, faculty and staff for student-related concerns
- Outreach presentations to the University and local community on a variety of emotional health topics

Emergency and After Hours Care
If students are experiencing a crisis or psychological emergency, they can call the CCPPS office at **304-293-4431** to speak with a counselor 24 hours a day, 7 days a week.

If a student or someone they know is feeling suicidal, the hotlines below can also provide assistance:
National Suicide Prevention Lifeline: 1-800-273-TALK (8255)
Military Veterans Suicide Hotline: 1-800-273-TALK (Press 1)
Trevor Project (LBGTQ): 1-866-4UTREVOR (1-866-488-7386)

How you can help a friend who is struggling: Kognito Interactive Training

Interact with student avatars in this online game.
Topics include:
- Techniques to talk to a friend you are concerned about
- How to recognize signs of distress
- What support services are available on your campus

For more information visit: well.wvu.edu/helpwell

Try it Today
- Go to: **https://www.kognitocampus.com/login/**
- Select "Create a New Account"
- Enter your information and use the proper enrollment key:
  Students – **wvu833**
  Staff & Faculty – **wvu664**
- Select a course and follow the on-screen instructions (30 minutes)

Office of Wellness & Health Promotion • 1st Floor • 304-293-5054 • well.wvu.edu/wellness

- liveWELL lifestyle educational series promotes positive wellbeing and academic performance decision making
- Academic offerings: Enhancing Wellbeing PE 293 N, Peer Education CHPR 260/261, and Yoga PE 203
- Open Yoga classes for students, faculty and staff
- HeartMath lab teaches students how to self-regulate their physiological stress response
- Farmers Market weekly in the Fall
- Sexual assault prevention, including the Green Dot bystander program
- leadWELL mentor program trains students to initiate health-related conversations with peers
- Student leadership opportunities: Student Wellness Ambassador Team (SWAT) members, RDVIC Peer Advocates, and leadWELL mentors
- Safe Communities Initiative: collaboration between Greater Morgantown and WVU to enhance safety and wellbeing

"At its best, the sensation of writing is that of any unmerited grace. It is handed to you, but only if you look for it. You search, you break your heart, your back, your brain, and then—and only then—it is handed to you."
—Annie Dillard

"The excellency of every art is its intensity, capable of making all disagreeables evaporate."
—John Keats

"Odd how the creative power at once brings the whole universe to order."
—Virginia Woolf

"Perhaps the truth depends on a walk around the lake."
—Wallace Stevens

Creative writing workshops at WVU will help you find the vital stories growing within you and learn to craft them in your voice through creative nonfiction, fiction, and poetry.

By Nathan Holmes

CHAPTER 1 What to Expect in English 101

OVERVIEW OF ENGLISH 101

English 101 is an introductory writing course designed to help you learn about writing so that you can use it as a major tool for success in college and beyond. While each English 101 instructor may use his or her own unique approach to teach the course, there are some core characteristics that all sections of English 101 have in common. Here's what you can expect:

English 101's Portfolio Approach

Writing is an ongoing process. To keep track of both your process and your progress over the course of the semester, you will collect all of your written work to create a portfolio of your writing. The portfolio emphasizes revision and encourages you to reflect on your work as a writer, reader, and thinker in English 101.

On the schedule of work due, you will see "final-for-now" deadlines for each of the four major projects in the course. Throughout the writing process, you will receive feedback from peers as well as your instructor.

All of the feedback you receive will help you make decisions about revising, editing, and proofreading your papers. There are two important things to know.

1. The feedback from your instructor will not include a letter grade.

Not receiving a grade on each paper will probably feel weird, but we do it for two reasons. First, we would rather evaluate your work based on what you've learned by the end of the course instead of evaluating your work while you're still practicing and learning. Second, we know from research and experience that students often stop writing once they receive a letter grade because a grade signals the end of the writing process. We want to give you the opportunity to keep working.

2. You will need to make decisions about your own work.

Writing can be a complex process. To get the most from this course, you need to take ownership of your work and make decisions about how to achieve your goals in writing. Your instructor will always be there to support and guide you, but your instructor cannot make those decisions for you. Therefore, you shouldn't expect your instructor's feedback to be a checklist for achieving an A. You must use all of your feedback to make decisions, apply all of your learning to all of your work, and demonstrate your knowledge of writing and rhetoric throughout your portfolio.

At mid-semester, you will be asked to create a mid-term portfolio. This is a practice attempt so that you can remedy any trouble spots before you hand in your final portfolio at the end of the term. This also gives your instructor an opportunity to provide you with an in-progress grade so that you have a realistic sense of where you stand in the course at the midpoint of the semester.

At the end of the semester, you will compile your final portfolio (see Chapter 7). The final portfolio is your chance to reflect on your work as a writer, reader, and thinker in English 101.

FOUR MAJOR PROJECTS AND PORTFOLIOS

Each English 101 class will ask you to complete four major projects that address four different purposes for writing. You will have the chance to develop each of your major projects through a process of getting started, shaping and drafting, reviewing and revising, and polishing and editing. You'll compose papers in and out of class, alone and in groups. These major projects will be the main content of your course portfolio. In total, you can expect to write 20 or more pages for your four major projects. This writing will comprise the biggest chunk of your portfolio, which counts for 70% of your final grade in the course.

For some of your writing, your instructor may ask you to bring enough draft copies to share with your group or will ask you to e-mail your papers to group members for an online workshop.

Portfolio Grades (70%). *To be eligible for full credit, each writer must meet all major deadlines throughout the semester. The final portfolio must show evidence of the writer's process by including the required reflective writing and at least one draft version of each and every major assignment in addition to the final portfolio versions.* Your final portfolio grade will be based on the following criteria:

A	**Superior portfolios** will demonstrate originality, initiative, and rhetorical sophistication that go beyond the requirements. A portfolio at this level is composed of well-edited texts of different genres that consistently show a clear, connected sense of audience, purpose, and development. The writer is able to analyze his or her own writing, reflect on it, and revise/rewrite accordingly. The portfolio takes risks that work.
B	In **strong portfolios**, the writing succeeds in meeting its rhetorical goals in terms of audience, purpose, and genre conventions without need for further major revisions of purpose, development, audience, or writing style/mechanics. The writer is able to reflect on his or her own writing and make some choices about revision. The writer takes risks, although they may not all be successful.
C	**Satisfactory portfolios** meet the basic requirements, yet the writing would benefit from further revisions of purpose, development, audience, or writing style/mechanics (or some combination) and a stronger understanding of rhetorical decision making. The writer composes across tasks at varying levels of success with some superficial revision. The writer has taken some risks in writing and exhibits some style.
D	**Weak portfolios** do not fully meet the basic evaluative standards. Most texts are brief and underdeveloped. These texts show a composing process that is not yet elaborated or reflective of rhetorical understanding. Texts generally require extensive revisions to address problems with purpose, development, audience, and/or writing style and mechanics.
F	**Unacceptable portfolios** exhibit pervasive problems with purpose, development, audience, or writing style/mechanics that interfere with meaning and readers' understanding. Unacceptable portfolios are often incomplete. A portfolio will also earn an F if it does not represent the writer's own original work.

EXPLORATORY WRITING

Exploratory writing is a means for experimenting with genre and style, as well as a means for thinking through responses to readings, writings, and class discussions. You'll be asked to write for a variety of purposes and in a variety of contexts—in class, asynchronous and synchronous communications (message boards, e-mail, and chat sessions), and at home—alone and in collaboration with others. Exploratory writing assignments may be 1 to 2 pages in length. You can expect to complete about 10 pages of this writing throughout the course.

Exploratory Writing (20%). Your exploratory writing grade will be based on the following criteria:

A	The writing is well developed, original, and succeeds in mastering new techniques and knowledge. The writing shows risks that work.
B	The writing has been done with considerable care and attention. It is developed and detailed.
C	The writing is acceptable. The student needs to spend more time or thought on the assignment.
D	The writing is unacceptable. It may be unfinished, inappropriate to the assignment, or written in class.
F	The student did not turn in any writing. (*Please note*: Late assignments are unacceptable.)

PARTICIPATION

This class employs active learning in order to have the greatest possible impact. This means that your attendance and active engagement in class are vital to the success of the course and your success. Participation includes showing up on time to class each day. It also means being prepared by bringing your textbooks and materials. Anything that inhibits your active participation or the active participation of your classmates can negatively affect your participation grade (e.g., texting, playing video games). Finally, participation includes meeting deadlines, bringing drafts for peer review, and making thoughtful contributions to classroom discussions. You can expect participation to count for 10% of your overall course grade.

Participation Grade (10%). Your participation grade will be based on the following criteria:

A	**Superior participation** shows initiative and excellence in written and verbal work. You were always well prepared and on time, and rarely, if ever, missed class. More than simply being present, you used writing, reading, and discussion as ways to study how you and others make choices about language and form, understand complex ideas, and connect with others. Reading and writing assignments were always completed with attention to detail. In workshop or conferences, suggestions to group members were tactful, thorough, specific, and often provided other student writers with a new perspective or insight.
B	**Strong participation** demonstrates active engagement in written and verbal work. You were always well prepared and on time, and rarely missed class. You played a consistently active role in large and small group discussions, even if your comments sometimes did not add *new* insights. Reading and writing assignments were completed with attention to detail, with only an occasional need for further development. In workshop or conferences, suggestions to group members were tactful, specific, and helpful.
C	**Satisfactory participation** demonstrates consistent written and verbal work that meets basic requirements. You made it to class prepared and on time, stayed focused on the day's work, and never exceeded the number of allowed absences. You met all deadlines for drafts of major assignments, reflective writing, and exploratory writing assignments. You contributed to small group workshops and large class discussions, but your written and verbal responses could often have benefited from more specific detail or more thoughtful development.
D	**Weak participation** demonstrates inconsistent written and verbal work. Some examples may include a pattern of being habitually late to class, missing more than the allowed number of classes, being unprepared for class, or being distracted during work (e.g., texting, surfing the Web, chatting on unrelated topics, etc.). Weak participation may also be characterized by infrequent or unproductive contributions to classroom discussions. Weak participation is also characterized by missing several writing deadlines. In workshops or conferences, suggestions to group members may have been missing, too brief and general to be of help, or too late to advance the discussion.
F	**Unacceptable participation** shows ineffectual written and verbal work. Some examples may include a pattern of being excessively late to class. Other examples may include missing most or all writing assignment deadlines and submitting work that fails to meet basic requirements. A pattern of being regularly unprepared made it impossible to contribute effectively to classroom discussions or small group workshops. In workshops or conferences, suggestions to group members may have been missing, too brief and general to be of help, disrespectful, or disruptive.

ENGLISH 101 POLICIES AND PROCEDURES

As you can see, English 101 involves you directly in writing, reading, researching, and responding. It is a class that encourages collaborative learning through small and large groups, formal and exploratory writing activities, and peer response and conference activities. Because the course depends on your active preparation for every class and your active involvement during every class meeting, regular and on-time attendance and active participation are critical to your success in this class. A productive and positive classroom community also depends on your responsibility and integrity. The following policies guide our expectations for the English 101 community.

Conferences

In addition to your regular class meetings, the English 101 curriculum uses small group and individual conferences to provide you with more direct instruction on your specific writing projects. During the semester, you can expect to meet for conferences with your instructor or with small groups of peers about three or four times. You can also expect that during a conference week, one regular class meeting will be cancelled in order to make room in the schedule for the conferences.

When you are meeting your instructor or peers for conferences, you should plan to bring the following:

- any questions you have about the current project
- your exploratory writing you have completed for the current project
- any drafting you have completed for the current project

Absences

We know that personal situations and required university events may, on a rare occasion, make it impossible for you to be in class. Remember, however, that's why a few absences are allowed; please reserve absences for emergencies.

- Students in all sections may miss one week of class without penalty.
- Students who miss more than one week of class may be penalized up to one letter grade for each additional absence.
- Students who miss more than three weeks of class will be assigned a failing grade for the course.

Note: In summer sessions, one week of class is defined as two class periods.

All absences (*including excused absences*) incurred from the date you register for the course will count toward the total number allowed. You are responsible for making up any work you may miss when you are not in class, even if the absence is necessitated by illness or personal emergency. This make-up work may include further exploratory writing, online work, telephone or e-mail collaboration, conferencing or peer review, and so on.

Please note: If you fail to turn in make-up assignments in a timely manner or if the make-up assignments are of insufficient quality, your instructor has the right to count your work as late or unacceptable.

Responsibilities When Absent for Illness, Injury, or Personal Emergency. If you have a contagious illness (such as the flu), severe injury, or a critical personal problem, you must, of course, take care of yourself. You do, however, have an obligation to notify your instructor as soon as possible, and you must arrange to make up any missed work in a timely fashion.

Responsibilities When Absent for University Activities or Religious Observance. In the case of university activities and religious observance, you must notify the instructor in writing *two weeks prior* to the date missed. You must arrange to complete all scheduled work.

Avoiding Extended Absences. If you know in advance that you will need to miss more than three consecutive class meetings, you should take the course in another term. It is much better for you as a writer and as a student to take the course during a semester when your schedule allows you to be present to do your best work.

Avoiding Habitual Lateness. Late arrivals disrupt the class. If some unusual circumstance makes you late on any given day, please be sure that you talk to your instructor after class. If you are habitually late to class, your instructor has the ability to record that repeated pattern as an absence. Please check with your instructor for specific details about the consequences associated with repeated lateness.

Attending Conferences. As part of this course, you will typically meet with your instructor for a conference three or four times each semester. It is particularly important for you to attend and be prepared for those meetings. Each conference will typically count as a full class day for attendance purposes.

Late Work

Late work is unacceptable and may affect your participation, exploratory writing, and portfolio writing grades.

If you are struggling with an assignment, if you are unexpectedly ill, or if you have some other personal emergency, contact your instructor immediately and you may be able to negotiate a special arrangement. Such arrangements are rare and require a formal, written request to your instructor that must include an explanation of the circumstances, documentation (if relevant), and a detailed plan for completing any late or missed work. Submitting a formal request does not automatically guarantee that the request will be granted.

Cheating/Plagiarism

The English 101 community assumes your honesty. Students are expected to be familiar with the sections on Academic Honesty in the University Student Conduct Code, Policy Bulletin 31, which is online at: http://campuslife.wvu.edu/office_of_student_conduct.

In English 101, we also expect students to submit their own *original* work. When you recycle your own past work or submit the same paper in more than one class, you are self-plagiarizing.

If you are repeating the class, you must talk to your instructor about whether you may use a previous assignment as the basis for further revisions.

If you are using a similar assignment for more than one class, permission must be obtained from the instructors of both classes. Permission is neither automatic nor guaranteed. Failure to disclose non-original or dual-submission work may result in an automatic F.

If you have any questions about when and how to document sources, or any other question that will help you avoid unintentional plagiarism (including self-plagiarism), please talk to your instructor. Plagiarism and cheating are serious offenses. Clear cases will result in an F for the course and appropriate academic discipline.

Document Retention

For your own records, make a photocopy, a back-up electronic copy, or other appropriate documentation of each project before submitting the original for review or evaluation. Technological glitches will occur, and it is *your responsibility* to be prepared for them. Because you will be asked to reflect on your progress throughout the semester, be sure to save all essays and projects that you complete.

Technology in the Classroom

Technology can often enhance class activities, but it can also be disruptive unless used responsibly. Please turn off your cell phones, put them out of sight, and refrain from texting in class. If the class is meeting in a computer classroom, please be sure you are using the computers only as instructed for that day's class session. If you are ever using technology in a way that is distracting or unrelated to the work of the class, you will be asked to put away the device or log off the computer. If your instructor has to discuss appropriate technology use with you more than once, you may be asked to leave and you will be counted as absent for that day. If there is an unusual circumstance where you must leave your phone on, please speak to your instructor privately *before* class.

Eberly Writing Studio

The Eberly Writing Studio is a resource that can help support you in all aspects of the writing process. It is located in G02 Colson Hall (the lower level). This is a free resource. You can meet with a tutor to go over the goals of any assignment or to get help brainstorming, organizing, or revising. The feedback from tutors will always focus on each writer's needs and abilities. Call 304-293-5788 to schedule an appointment or stop by to see if a tutor is available. Their website is http://speakwrite.wvu.edu/writing-studio.

University Counseling Services

The Carruth Center provides resources to help manage stress, improve relationships, make healthy lifestyle choices, and face new challenges and transitions. They have drop-in hours as well as scheduled programs and appointments. You'll find the Carruth Center on the third floor of the Student Services Building, right next door to the Mountainlair. Their hours are Monday–Friday, 8:15 A.M.–4:45 P.M. Their phone number (answered 24 hours) is 304-293-4431. Their website is http://well.wvu.edu/ccpps.

Writing Course Concerns

In the event that you have a concern about your class or your assignments, please talk to your instructor. Most conflicts or concerns are best resolved through direct communication between the instructor and student.

If you still have a concern after talking to your instructor, please see Mary Vasquez in the main English office (100 Colson Hall) to get a Writing Course Concern form. This form asks you to identify the nature of your concern or complaint and suggest a resolution to the problem. This form helps the writing program administrators respond to student concerns in an organized and timely way. You can usually expect a response to your concern within two working days from the time it is received (and always within five working days).

COMPUTER CLASSROOM BEST PRACTICES

As a student in the computer classroom, and using the computer to contribute to discussions outside of class, I commit to the following:

- During the class period, to use only websites that are relevant for class work or that the teacher has directed me to use;
- To recognize that my attention must be given to my teacher and not the computer when I am directed;
- To pay attention to teacher instruction and take notes so that I remember how to navigate the websites and programs we will be using in class;
- To be respectful of other students' opinions and work as I respond to discussion postings or in peer review;
- To be sure that assignments posted or submitted for class have uploaded or attached properly. I recognize that "I didn't know it didn't post" is not a legitimate excuse for late work;
- To make sure that I have posted my assignment or discussion points in the proper thread;
- To post or submit my assignments on time with the recognition that if the post time is after assignment due time, my assignment is considered late;
- To be sure to save and submit documents only as Microsoft Word 97–2003 .doc files or, if this isn't possible, as .rtf files;
- To take responsibility for bringing all files to class when they are needed—I cannot ever use lab printers;
- To take responsibility for saving multiple versions of all files and documents, so that I never lose an important assignment—if I lose a file or a computer crashes, it is my responsibility to have backed my data up;
- To back up my files, I will routinely e-mail files to myself, save them on multiple drives, and so on;
- To understand that if I have been asked to bring a print copy of an assignment to class, I need to print this assignment myself and bring it in;
- To ask questions if I am confused about how to navigate or use the computer programs the teacher is using during class—no one is expected to be an expert;
- To refrain from bringing food or drink into the classroom;
- To leave the lab as I found it (pushed-in chairs, without garbage, leftover handouts, etc., left in the lab);
- To report any problems with technology right away so that they can be quickly fixed.

COURSE GOALS FOR ENGLISH 101

NOTES

The undergraduate writing program at West Virginia University has developed a set of four course goals that all of our instructors use to guide our teaching. These goals are based on the "Outcomes Statement for First-Year Composition" published by the Council of Writing Program Administrators.

Goal 1: Rhetoric—Identify and interpret communication situations, goals, and audiences

Goal 2: Inquiry—Explore and analyze ideas through reading and composing

Goal 3: Processes—Demonstrate processes for composing and research

Goal 4: Conventions—Recognize and use writing conventions appropriate for various contexts

NOTES

Goal 1: Rhetoric

When writing teachers encourage you to understand the rhetorical situation of your writing, they are referring to factors such as purpose, audience, conventions, and trouble spots. For example, when you write an e-mail to a friend, you probably automatically run through this list without thinking much about it. You might use the e-mail's subject line to explain why you are writing. You might reference a joke or an experience you know your friend will understand. You might use conventions of informal writing like LOL or ICYMI to communicate an idea. You might even change a word or a phrase to avoid having your friend misinterpret you. These are all important elements of rhetorical situations.

By the end of 101, you should be able to:

- Identify and describe the important components of a rhetorical situation
- Focus on a purpose for writing and understand what form your writing should take depending on the rhetorical situation
- Apply your understanding of rhetoric to your choices as a writer
- Understand what it means to write for an "audience" and be able to express how different audiences might have different expectations for your writing

Take a minute to write down some things you already know about rhetoric.

NOTES

Goal 2: Inquiry

In the context of English 101, we think it's important for you to be able to use writing and reading as a way to explore, to analyze, and to reflect.

By the end of 101, you should be able to:

- Reflect on your abilities and progress
- Self-assess
- Use writing for diverse purposes, including inquiry, exploration, problem solving, thinking, and communicating
- Use a variety of research strategies (field research, interviews, web research, and some library research—although you'll do more of that in 102)
- Select and use evidence effectively to contextualize and support your purposes for writing

In what ways have you used inquiry in the past to investigate something or do research?

NOTES

Goal 3: Processes

Writing is a process. That means it takes more than one step to produce writing. Even writing a short e-mail in less than 5 minutes may involve processes like looking up information, writing sentences, editing sentences by using your mouse and the delete key, reading what you wrote to make sure it sounds right, and so on. All of these processes happen before you press the send key. All of these steps might not happen in the same order every time. Sometimes, you might even need to repeat steps to get your writing done. This course will help you identify the steps in your writing process, add valuable steps that can help you, and help you sort out when to do what and how to do it.

By the end of 101, you should be able to:

- Engage in flexible strategies for inventing, drafting, revising, editing, and proofreading
- Collaborate with others to give and receive effective feedback
- Identify what processes work best for you as a writer
- Assess and use relevant technologies for communication and research

Describe your writing process. What works for you?

NOTES

Goal 4: Conventions

In the context of writing, when we talk about *conventions* we simply mean "the way things are typically done." As a communicator, it is important that you know the underlying "rules" of writing. One part of that knowledge comes from being aware of the traits that distinguish one type of writing from another (different types are called different genres). A second part is giving credit to others when you use their ideas and language to support your own writing. We typically do that through things like in-text citations and works cited pages. Finally, a third part of understanding conventions means being able to control features such as punctuation and spelling. Because there are a lot of these rules to remember, it's also important that you're aware of what resources you have to use when you *don't* know the rules.

By the end of 101, you should be able to:

- Identify and write in different genres for different rhetorical situations
- Employ appropriate conventions for different genres, including the documentation of sources and surface features like punctuation and spelling
- Use an academic citation system like MLA for documenting work

To help you achieve these goals, we have also developed the following worksheets. We've included four of each sheet for you in the textbook so that you have one for each major project. We encourage you to use them for each project; however, you might choose to save one for photocopying so that you can use these sheets in other classes for other projects.

NOTES

Purpose

What exactly do I want to happen?

The **purpose** is what you want to accomplish or the reason for communicating. After figuring out your topic (what you are communicating about) and angle (point or theme)—*what* you are writing about, you should try clearly stating your purpose—*why* you are writing.

WHAT IS YOUR REASON FOR COMMUNICATING?

(Put a star next to your primary purpose and put a check mark next to all other possibilities.)

- expressing ideas
- informing someone
- explaining something
- exploring a topic
- persuading someone

QUESTIONS TO CONSIDER

1. What do you hope your audience will do, feel, or think after experiencing this communication?

___

___

___

2. Is there an event or situation that made you want to communicate?

___

___

___

3. What is the best possible outcome of this communication?

___

___

___

4. What is the worst possible outcome?

___

___

___

For more information, refer to page ____ or consult *speakwrite.wvu.edu.*

Purpose

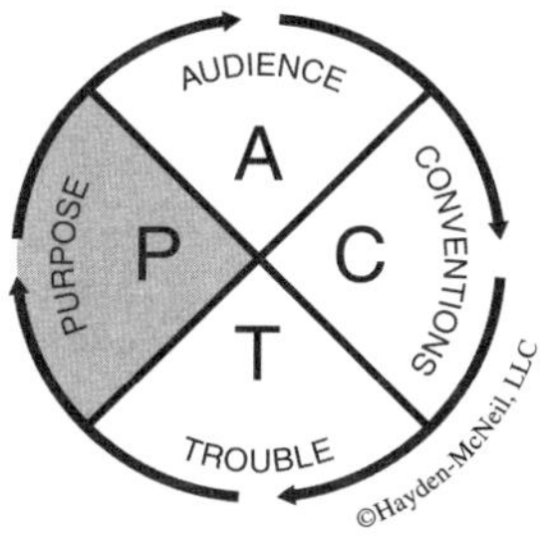

What exactly do I want to happen?

The **purpose** is what you want to accomplish or the reason for communicating. After figuring out your topic (what you are communicating about) and angle (point or theme)—*what* you are writing about, you should try clearly stating your purpose—*why* you are writing.

WHAT IS YOUR REASON FOR COMMUNICATING?

(Put a star next to your primary purpose and put a check mark next to all other possibilities.)

- expressing ideas
- informing someone
- explaining something
- exploring a topic
- persuading someone

QUESTIONS TO CONSIDER

1. What do you hope your audience will do, feel, or think after experiencing this communication?

____

____

____

2. Is there an event or situation that made you want to communicate?

____

____

____

3. What is the best possible outcome of this communication?

____

____

____

4. What is the worst possible outcome?

____

____

____

For more information, refer to page ____ or consult *speakwrite.wvu.edu.*

Purpose

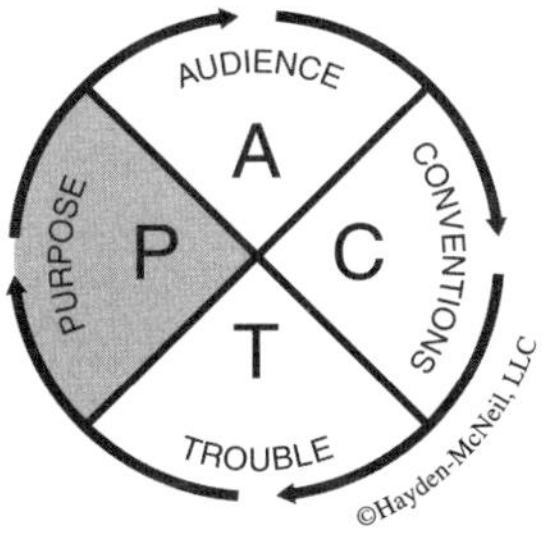

What exactly do I want to happen?

The **purpose** is what you want to accomplish or the reason for communicating. After figuring out your topic (what you are communicating about) and angle (point or theme)—*what* you are writing about, you should try clearly stating your purpose—*why* you are writing.

WHAT IS YOUR REASON FOR COMMUNICATING?

(Put a star next to your primary purpose and put a check mark next to all other possibilities.)

- expressing ideas
- informing someone
- explaining something
- exploring a topic
- persuading someone

QUESTIONS TO CONSIDER

1. What do you hope your audience will do, feel, or think after experiencing this communication?

____

____

____

2. Is there an event or situation that made you want to communicate?

____

____

____

3. What is the best possible outcome of this communication?

____

____

____

4. What is the worst possible outcome?

____

____

____

For more information, refer to page ____ or consult *speakwrite.wvu.edu.*

Purpose

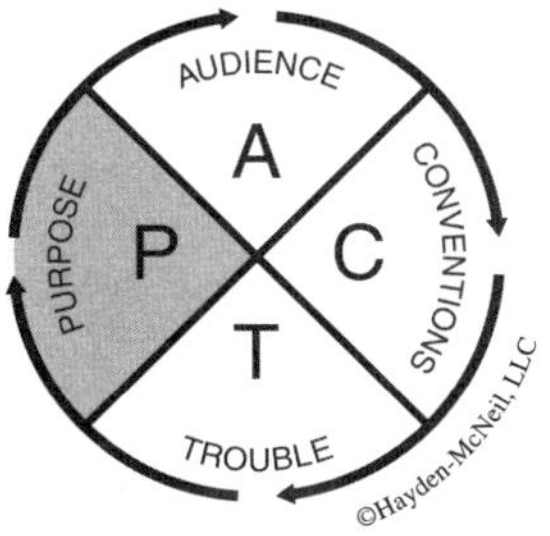

What exactly do I want to happen?

The **purpose** is what you want to accomplish or the reason for communicating. After figuring out your topic (what you are communicating about) and angle (point or theme)—*what* you are writing about, you should try clearly stating your purpose—*why* you are writing.

WHAT IS YOUR REASON FOR COMMUNICATING?

(Put a star next to your primary purpose and put a check mark next to all other possibilities.)

- expressing ideas
- informing someone
- explaining something
- exploring a topic
- persuading someone

QUESTIONS TO CONSIDER

1. What do you hope your audience will do, feel, or think after experiencing this communication?

___

___

___

2. Is there an event or situation that made you want to communicate?

___

___

___

3. What is the best possible outcome of this communication?

___

___

___

4. What is the worst possible outcome?

___

___

___

For more information, refer to page ____ or consult *speakwrite.wvu.edu.*

Audience

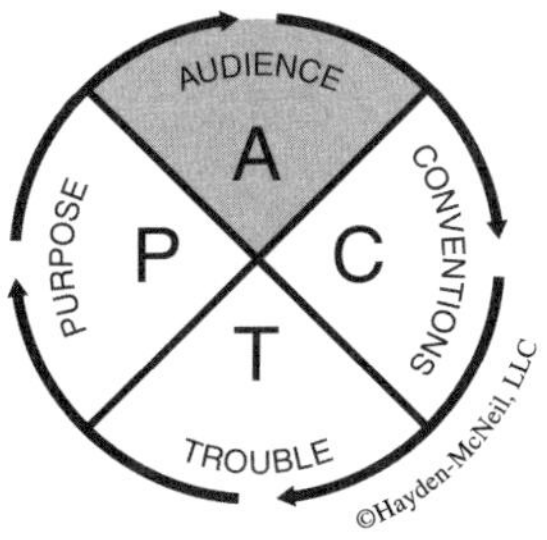

Who is reading, listening, or viewing?

The **audience** is who you are addressing. The qualities of an audience contribute to how they read and understand. A communicator must recognize that audiences are not one dimensional and that there are multiple types of audiences.

TYPES OF AUDIENCES TO CONSIDER

1. Primary: The audience the communicator intends to influence.
2. Secondary: The audience that the primary audience turns to for advice.
3. Tertiary: The unintended audience.

CONSIDER YOUR PRIMARY AUDIENCE'S:	CHECK THE MOST IMPORTANT (FOR YOUR TEXT)	EXPLANATION
Age		
Gender		
Ethnicity		
Level of education		
Sexual orientation		
Class		
Upbringing		
Place of living		
Place of work		
Emotional status (tired, angry, receptive…)		
Past experience with the topic/issue/matter		
Values/beliefs/commitments relative to the topic/issue/matter		
Self-identify: the kinds of relations people see themselves having with others (mother ± unemployed ± worker ± student ± teacher ± ???)		

For more information, refer to page ____ or consult *speakwrite.wvu.edu.*

Audience

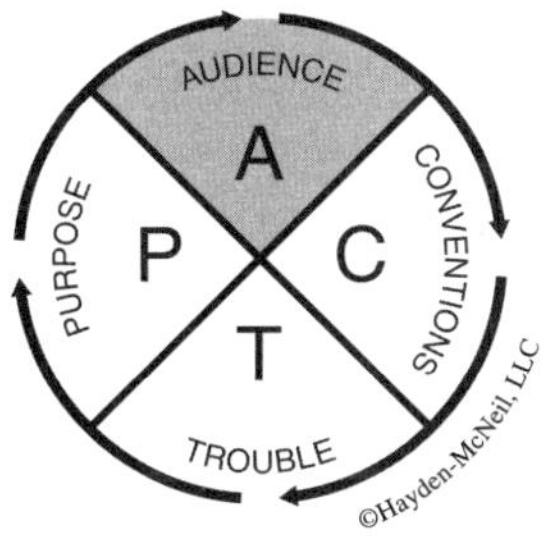

Who is reading, listening, or viewing?

The **audience** is who you are addressing. The qualities of an audience contribute to how they read and understand. A communicator must recognize that audiences are not one dimensional and that there are multiple types of audiences.

TYPES OF AUDIENCES TO CONSIDER

1. Primary: The audience the communicator intends to influence.
2. Secondary: The audience that the primary audience turns to for advice.
3. Tertiary: The unintended audience.

CONSIDER YOUR PRIMARY AUDIENCE'S:	CHECK THE MOST IMPORTANT (FOR YOUR TEXT)	EXPLANATION
Age		
Gender		
Ethnicity		
Level of education		
Sexual orientation		
Class		
Upbringing		
Place of living		
Place of work		
Emotional status (tired, angry, receptive…)		
Past experience with the topic/issue/matter		
Values/beliefs/commitments relative to the topic/issue/matter		
Self-identify: the kinds of relations people see themselves having with others (mother ± unemployed ± worker ± student ± teacher ± ???)		

For more information, refer to page ____ or consult *speakwrite.wvu.edu.*

Audience

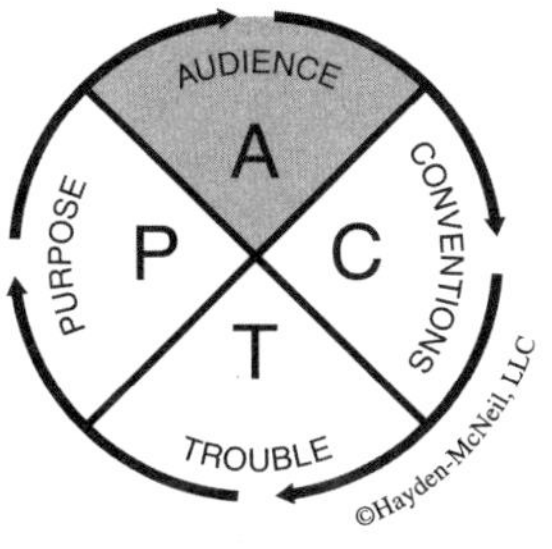

Who is reading, listening, or viewing?

The **audience** is who you are addressing. The qualities of an audience contribute to how they read and understand. A communicator must recognize that audiences are not one dimensional and that there are multiple types of audiences.

TYPES OF AUDIENCES TO CONSIDER

1. Primary: The audience the communicator intends to influence.
2. Secondary: The audience that the primary audience turns to for advice.
3. Tertiary: The unintended audience.

CONSIDER YOUR PRIMARY AUDIENCE'S:	CHECK THE MOST IMPORTANT (FOR YOUR TEXT)	EXPLANATION
Age		
Gender		
Ethnicity		
Level of education		
Sexual orientation		
Class		
Upbringing		
Place of living		
Place of work		
Emotional status (tired, angry, receptive…)		
Past experience with the topic/issue/matter		
Values/beliefs/commitments relative to the topic/issue/matter		
Self-identify: the kinds of relations people see themselves having with others (mother ± unemployed ± worker ± student ± teacher ± ???)		

For more information, refer to page ____ or consult *speakwrite.wvu.edu.*

Audience

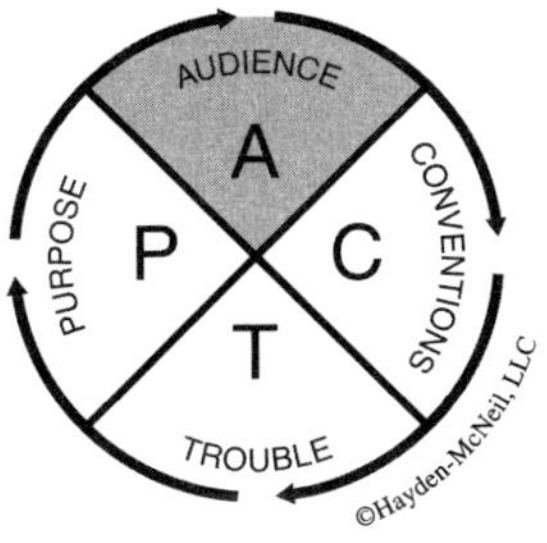

Who is reading, listening, or viewing?

The **audience** is who you are addressing. The qualities of an audience contribute to how they read and understand. A communicator must recognize that audiences are not one dimensional and that there are multiple types of audiences.

TYPES OF AUDIENCES TO CONSIDER

1. Primary: The audience the communicator intends to influence.
2. Secondary: The audience that the primary audience turns to for advice.
3. Tertiary: The unintended audience.

CONSIDER YOUR PRIMARY AUDIENCE'S:	CHECK THE MOST IMPORTANT (FOR YOUR TEXT)	EXPLANATION
Age		
Gender		
Ethnicity		
Level of education		
Sexual orientation		
Class		
Upbringing		
Place of living		
Place of work		
Emotional status (tired, angry, receptive…)		
Past experience with the topic/issue/matter		
Values/beliefs/commitments relative to the topic/issue/matter		
Self-identify: the kinds of relations people see themselves having with others (mother ± unemployed ± worker ± student ± teacher ± ???)		

For more information, refer to page ____ or consult *speakwrite.wvu.edu*.

Conventions

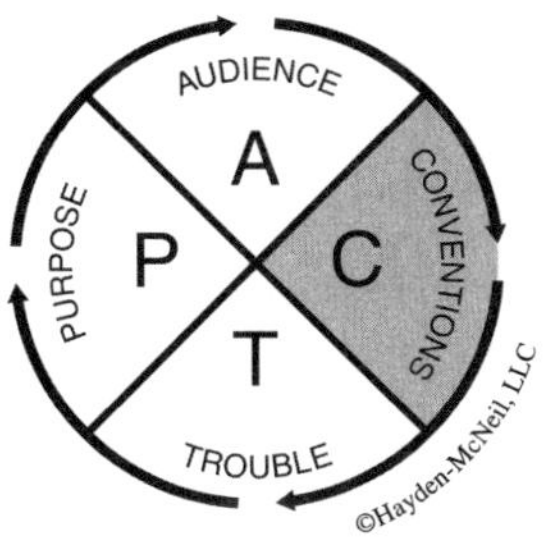

What is expected in this context?

The **conventions** are what is expected and what is appropriate in a specific genre. Describe what you are composing on the lines provided. Next use the MLA checklist below to brainstorm about the conventions of your document. For example, is your document double-spaced like an MLA-formatted paper or is it different?

MLA BASIC CONVENTIONS

- Typed and on standard, white 8.5 × 11-inch paper with 1-inch margins.
- Double-spaced, 12 pt. Times New Roman font.
- Indent the first line of paragraphs.
- List your name, your instructor's name, the course, and the date in the upper left-hand corner of your first page.
- Create a header that includes your last name and numbers all pages consecutively in the upper right-hand corner.
- Center the title. (Do not underline, italicize, or put quotation marks in your title.)
- Use italics throughout your essay for the titles of larger works (books, magazines) and quotation marks for titles of shorter works (poems, articles).

MLA BASIC WORKS CITED CONVENTIONS

- The Works Cited page is on a separate page at the end of the paper.
- Create a hanging indent.
- List entries in alphabetical order.

MLA BASIC IN-TEXT CITATIONS

- MLA follows the author-page method of in-text citation, meaning that the author's last name and the page number or numbers that are used must appear in the text.

  Example: (Franklin 476)
- The author's name appears in the sentence itself or in the parentheses following the quotation, paraphrase, or summary.

  Example: According to Franklin, *insert quote, paraphrase, or summary* (476).
- Remember that quotes cannot stand alone!

For more information, refer to page ____ or consult *speakwrite.wvu.edu*.

Conventions

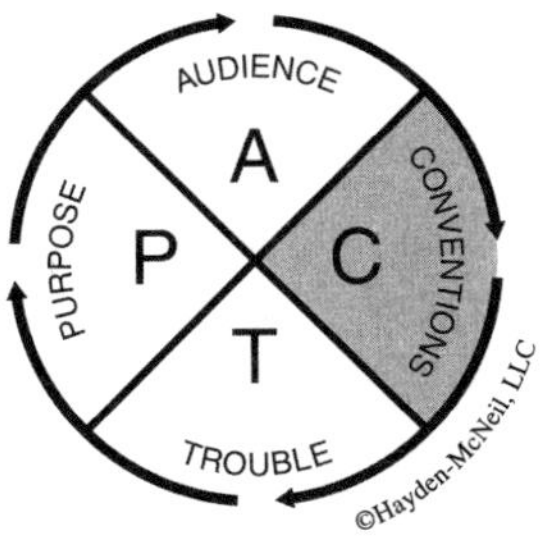

What is expected in this context?

The **conventions** are what is expected and what is appropriate in a specific genre. Describe what you are composing on the lines provided. Next use the MLA checklist below to brainstorm about the conventions of your document. For example, is your document double-spaced like an MLA-formatted paper or is it different?

MLA BASIC CONVENTIONS

- Typed and on standard, white 8.5 × 11-inch paper with 1-inch margins.
- Double-spaced, 12 pt. Times New Roman font.
- Indent the first line of paragraphs.
- List your name, your instructor's name, the course, and the date in the upper left-hand corner of your first page.
- Create a header that includes your last name and numbers all pages consecutively in the upper right-hand corner.
- Center the title. (Do not underline, italicize, or put quotation marks in your title.)
- Use italics throughout your essay for the titles of larger works (books, magazines) and quotation marks for titles of shorter works (poems, articles).

MLA BASIC WORKS CITED CONVENTIONS

- The Works Cited page is on a separate page at the end of the paper.
- Create a hanging indent.
- List entries in alphabetical order.

MLA BASIC IN-TEXT CITATIONS

- MLA follows the author-page method of in-text citation, meaning that the author's last name and the page number or numbers that are used must appear in the text.

  Example: (Franklin 476)

- The author's name appears in the sentence itself or in the parentheses following the quotation, paraphrase, or summary.

  Example: According to Franklin, *insert quote, paraphrase, or summary* (476).

- Remember that quotes cannot stand alone!

For more information, refer to page ____ or consult *speakwrite.wvu.edu.*

Conventions

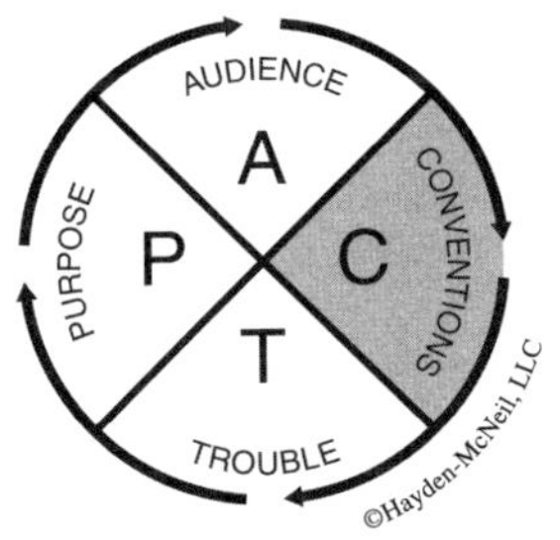

What is expected in this context?

The **conventions** are what is expected and what is appropriate in a specific genre. Describe what you are composing on the lines provided. Next use the MLA checklist below to brainstorm about the conventions of your document. For example, is your document double-spaced like an MLA-formatted paper or is it different?

MLA BASIC CONVENTIONS

- Typed and on standard, white 8.5 × 11-inch paper with 1-inch margins.
- Double-spaced, 12 pt. Times New Roman font.
- Indent the first line of paragraphs.
- List your name, your instructor's name, the course, and the date in the upper left-hand corner of your first page.
- Create a header that includes your last name and numbers all pages consecutively in the upper right-hand corner.
- Center the title. (Do not underline, italicize, or put quotation marks in your title.)
- Use italics throughout your essay for the titles of larger works (books, magazines) and quotation marks for titles of shorter works (poems, articles).

MLA BASIC WORKS CITED CONVENTIONS

- The Works Cited page is on a separate page at the end of the paper.
- Create a hanging indent.
- List entries in alphabetical order.

MLA BASIC IN-TEXT CITATIONS

- MLA follows the author-page method of in-text citation, meaning that the author's last name and the page number or numbers that are used must appear in the text.

  Example: (Franklin 476)

- The author's name appears in the sentence itself or in the parentheses following the quotation, paraphrase, or summary.

  Example: According to Franklin, *insert quote, paraphrase, or summary* (476).

- Remember that quotes cannot stand alone!

For more information, refer to page ____ or consult *speakwrite.wvu.edu.*

Conventions

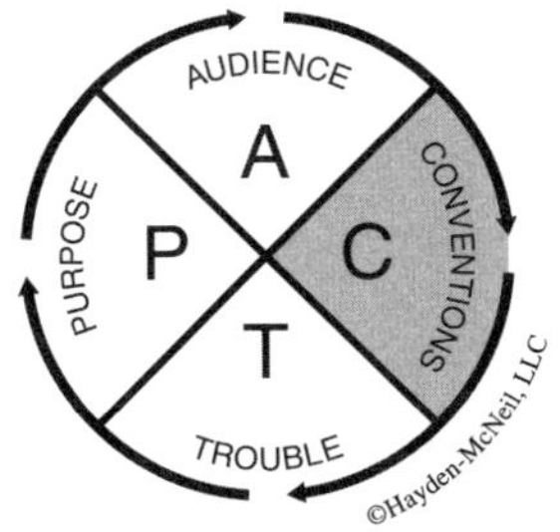

What is expected in this context?

The **conventions** are what is expected and what is appropriate in a specific genre. Describe what you are composing on the lines provided. Next use the MLA checklist below to brainstorm about the conventions of your document. For example, is your document double-spaced like an MLA-formatted paper or is it different?

____

____

____

____

MLA BASIC CONVENTIONS

- Typed and on standard, white 8.5 × 11-inch paper with 1-inch margins.
- Double-spaced, 12 pt. Times New Roman font.
- Indent the first line of paragraphs.
- List your name, your instructor's name, the course, and the date in the upper left-hand corner of your first page.
- Create a header that includes your last name and numbers all pages consecutively in the upper right-hand corner.
- Center the title. (Do not underline, italicize, or put quotation marks in your title.)
- Use italics throughout your essay for the titles of larger works (books, magazines) and quotation marks for titles of shorter works (poems, articles).

MLA BASIC WORKS CITED CONVENTIONS

- The Works Cited page is on a separate page at the end of the paper.
- Create a hanging indent.
- List entries in alphabetical order.

MLA BASIC IN-TEXT CITATIONS

- MLA follows the author-page method of in-text citation, meaning that the author's last name and the page number or numbers that are used must appear in the text.

  Example: (Franklin 476)
- The author's name appears in the sentence itself or in the parentheses following the quotation, paraphrase, or summary.

  Example: According to Franklin, *insert quote, paraphrase, or summary* (476).
- Remember that quotes cannot stand alone!

For more information, refer to page ____ or consult *speakwrite.wvu.edu*.

Trouble Spots

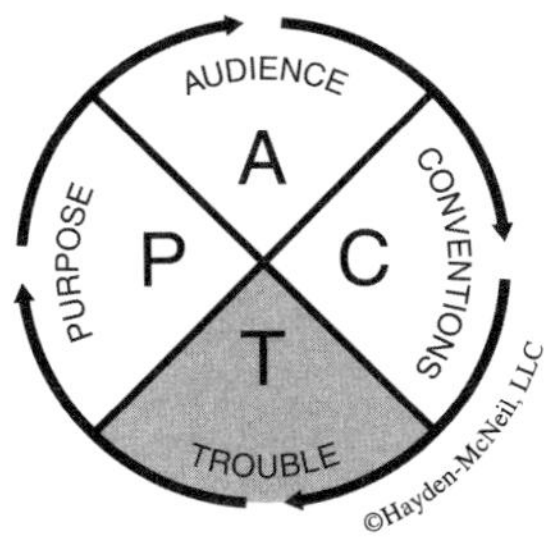

What could get in the way of my goals?

The **trouble spots** include anything that can keep you from effectively conveying your purpose, accounting for your audience, and carrying out appropriate and necessary conventions. Use the checklist below when you have completed your assignment.

PURPOSE

- Is there a title? Is it misleading?
- Do I establish *ethos*?
- Is my thesis statement strong and clear? Does it convey the purpose?
- Does the audience do, think, or feel what I want them to after this communication?
- Do I have a catchy introduction?
- Have I effectively carried out my reason for communicating (persuade, inform, etc.)?

AUDIENCE

- Am I using the correct level of formality?
- Do I explain terms or concepts?
- Have I considered that audiences are dynamic rather than one dimensional?
- Do I recognize that audiences' qualities will contribute to how they read and understand?
- Have I considered secondary or tertiary audiences or who else might be reading this?

CONVENTIONS

- Am I using the appropriate conventions (letter, memo, research paper)?
- Do I use and follow the guidelines of MLA formatting?
- Am I avoiding plagiarism (citations and works cited)?
- Have I checked the requirements of the assignment? Do I understand them?
- Have I asked questions for clarification when needed?
- What do I know that I need help with (spelling, grammar, thesis, organization)?
- Have I read over my paper? More than once?
- Has someone else read over my paper?

For more information, refer to page ____ or consult *speakwrite.wvu.edu.*

Trouble Spots

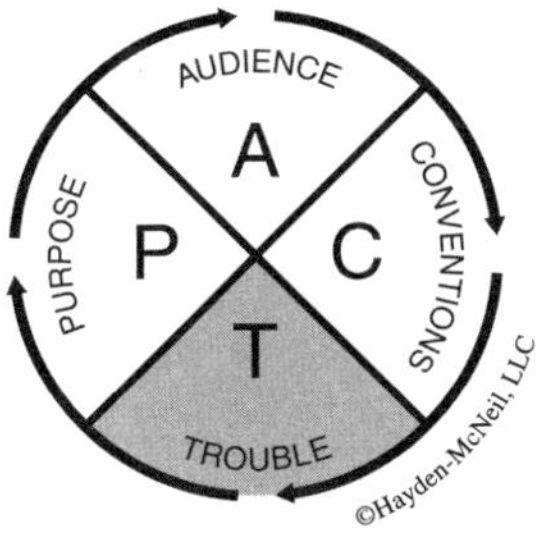

What could get in the way of my goals?

The **trouble spots** include anything that can keep you from effectively conveying your purpose, accounting for your audience, and carrying out appropriate and necessary conventions. Use the checklist below when you have completed your assignment.

PURPOSE

- Is there a title? Is it misleading?
- Do I establish *ethos*?
- Is my thesis statement strong and clear? Does it convey the purpose?
- Does the audience do, think, or feel what I want them to after this communication?
- Do I have a catchy introduction?
- Have I effectively carried out my reason for communicating (persuade, inform, etc.)?

AUDIENCE

- Am I using the correct level of formality?
- Do I explain terms or concepts?
- Have I considered that audiences are dynamic rather than one dimensional?
- Do I recognize that audiences' qualities will contribute to how they read and understand?
- Have I considered secondary or tertiary audiences or who else might be reading this?

CONVENTIONS

- Am I using the appropriate conventions (letter, memo, research paper)?
- Do I use and follow the guidelines of MLA formatting?
- Am I avoiding plagiarism (citations and works cited)?
- Have I checked the requirements of the assignment? Do I understand them?
- Have I asked questions for clarification when needed?
- What do I know that I need help with (spelling, grammar, thesis, organization)?
- Have I read over my paper? More than once?
- Has someone else read over my paper?

For more information, refer to page ____ or consult *speakwrite.wvu.edu.*

Trouble Spots

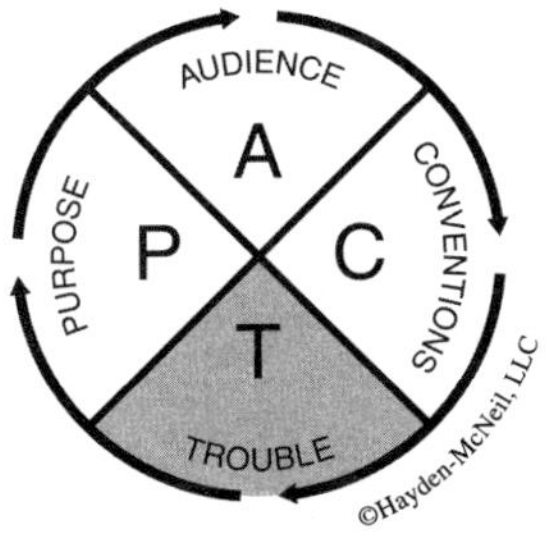

What could get in the way of my goals?

The **trouble spots** include anything that can keep you from effectively conveying your purpose, accounting for your audience, and carrying out appropriate and necessary conventions. Use the checklist below when you have completed your assignment.

PURPOSE

- Is there a title? Is it misleading?
- Do I establish *ethos*?
- Is my thesis statement strong and clear? Does it convey the purpose?
- Does the audience do, think, or feel what I want them to after this communication?
- Do I have a catchy introduction?
- Have I effectively carried out my reason for communicating (persuade, inform, etc.)?

AUDIENCE

- Am I using the correct level of formality?
- Do I explain terms or concepts?
- Have I considered that audiences are dynamic rather than one dimensional?
- Do I recognize that audiences' qualities will contribute to how they read and understand?
- Have I considered secondary or tertiary audiences or who else might be reading this?

CONVENTIONS

- Am I using the appropriate conventions (letter, memo, research paper)?
- Do I use and follow the guidelines of MLA formatting?
- Am I avoiding plagiarism (citations and works cited)?
- Have I checked the requirements of the assignment? Do I understand them?
- Have I asked questions for clarification when needed?
- What do I know that I need help with (spelling, grammar, thesis, organization)?
- Have I read over my paper? More than once?
- Has someone else read over my paper?

For more information, refer to page ____ or consult *speakwrite.wvu.edu.*

Trouble Spots

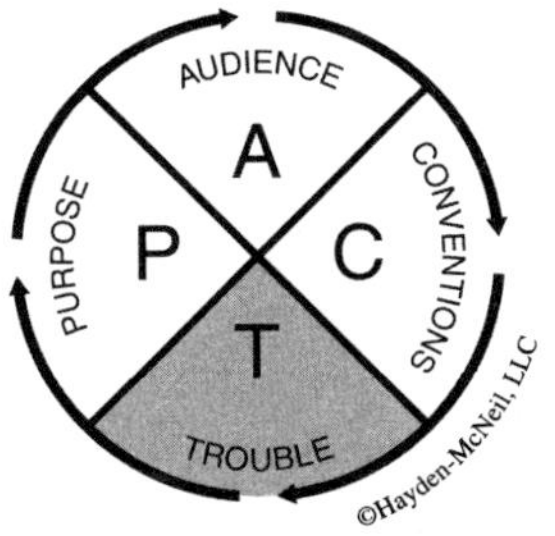

What could get in the way of my goals?

The **trouble spots** include anything that can keep you from effectively conveying your purpose, accounting for your audience, and carrying out appropriate and necessary conventions. Use the checklist below when you have completed your assignment.

PURPOSE

- Is there a title? Is it misleading?
- Do I establish *ethos*?
- Is my thesis statement strong and clear? Does it convey the purpose?
- Does the audience do, think, or feel what I want them to after this communication?
- Do I have a catchy introduction?
- Have I effectively carried out my reason for communicating (persuade, inform, etc.)?

AUDIENCE

- Am I using the correct level of formality?
- Do I explain terms or concepts?
- Have I considered that audiences are dynamic rather than one dimensional?
- Do I recognize that audiences' qualities will contribute to how they read and understand?
- Have I considered secondary or tertiary audiences or who else might be reading this?

CONVENTIONS

- Am I using the appropriate conventions (letter, memo, research paper)?
- Do I use and follow the guidelines of MLA formatting?
- Am I avoiding plagiarism (citations and works cited)?
- Have I checked the requirements of the assignment? Do I understand them?
- Have I asked questions for clarification when needed?
- What do I know that I need help with (spelling, grammar, thesis, organization)?
- Have I read over my paper? More than once?
- Has someone else read over my paper?

For more information, refer to page ____ or consult *speakwrite.wvu.edu.*

CHAPTER 2
Writing to Tell Your Story

We begin the major writing in English 101 by asking you to write a story. In some ways, this project is easy. In other ways, it may be the hardest project you face the whole term.

GETTING STARTED

Overview of Project: Writing to Tell Your Story

PURPOSE

The purpose of this assignment is to practice important elements of writing like description and organization.

GENRE

One common genre for this type of writing is the literacy narrative. Typically, these narratives describe key moments in an author's life that led to reading and writing.

AUDIENCE

Your instructor may have specific instructions about what audience to write for. Otherwise, consider writing for an audience of people who match you in terms of race, gender, ethnicity, and/or religion.

ORGANIZATION

There are countless ways that authors organize stories. Listen for your instructor to give you specific instructions about how to organize your story. Possibilities often include flashbacks, multiple genres, or even multiple perspectives.

NOTES

ASSESSMENT

Your instructor may adjust the criteria below to fit the specific project for your course. In any case, here are a few key criteria to keep in mind:

- Use a narrative base (in other words, your writing sounds like a story)
- Convey a personal experience in a way that is interesting and relevant to an audience
- Select and use descriptive detail and examples appropriate to your purpose(s) and audience(s)
- Convey some source of tension in the story that eventually turns toward a resolution
- Reflect on the new perspective you have gained since the experience
- Produce approximately 1,200 to 1,500 words (4–5 pages) of polished writing

TURNING IT IN

The assignment is due: ____________________

I need to ____

____

____

NOTES

FREEWRITING

Freewriting is an activity meant to help you come up with ideas and record them. Despite how it sounds, there are actually two rules for freewriting that will help you get the most out of the activity:

1. **Do not worry about spelling, grammar, and punctuation.** That's right! Forget about all that stuff that slows you down, makes you worry your writing isn't good, or causes you to pause every 10 seconds and reread what you wrote. Just write. Focus on getting the ideas down on the page.
2. **Do not stop writing.** This is the part that gets people. We often have a tendency to stop writing when an idea or a sentence ends, and we're trying to think of what to write next. When you're freewriting, you want to fight this urge. Keep writing even if you have to write, "I don't know what to write next" five times. Keep going until a new idea pops out.

OK, are you ready? Try a short freewrite for 3 minutes on this page. Here's a simple prompt to help you:

Write about writing for 3 minutes. Write down everything you know or want to know about writing. You can even include how you feel about writing and why.

Ready. Set. Go.

How did it go? Freewriting can feel kind of awkward at first if you're not used to doing it. Just remember that freewriting is a great way to get some ideas flowing for a new project or for a paper you're stuck on. It can be a useful tool. It's also an activity that we would categorize under invention. In writing, **invention** is a term we use to talk about how we come up with new ideas. We'll address invention even more in the chapters to come.

NOTES

ANNOTATING A TEXT

Have you ever read a magazine article or a textbook chapter for school, gotten to the end of it, and asked yourself, "What did I just read?" Or maybe you go to the library, pull out your highlighter, and then highlight every single word because it all seems so important. Reading, understanding, and remembering a piece of writing can be a tough job.

To help with this, it is important to develop strategies for annotating a text. To annotate simply means that you "add notes or comments" to something ("Annotate").* There is no one, correct way to annotate a text, but you may find it helpful to have a system. Try some of the ideas below and see what works best for you.

- Use two different colored highlighters. Use one color to highlight the author's claims and another to highlight the author's evidence.
- Use a pen to underline the most important sentence in each paragraph.
- Write questions in the margin when you get confused or need more information.

For more on annotating a text, look at pages 36 and 37 in *Easy Writer*.

---

* Pssst! Down here. In the writing above, we quoted a definition from the *Merriam-Webster Dictionary*, and we included an in-text citation for it. This might be helpful if you ever quote a dictionary definition in your own work. Check the Works Cited section at the back of this book to see an example of how to cite a dictionary definition.

NOTES

Activity: Reading Like a Writer

While we often read for pleasure or to learn a new concept, one thing is for certain—reading is inherently linked to writing; you can't do one without the other. As students of writing, try to read like a writer and notice the techniques that other writers use. Practice some of the techniques below using the sample essay at the end of this chapter.

- Look at the title of the work. What do you expect before you read? Once you have finished reading, take another look at the title. Is it effective? How do titles keep their readers in mind? Can you suggest an alternative title? What title will you give your own narrative? Try brainstorming a few ideas.
- How does the writer use detail, imagery, metaphor, structure, voice, style, point of view, verb tense, headings, dialogue, images, other documents, organization, plot? List a few specific techniques you admire in the text you are reading.
- Find a single passage that catches your attention in some way. How did the author achieve this effect? How did she/he make this technique work?
- As you read, look for one or two techniques that you admire or that you've *never* tried before. How might you take a similar risk in your own writing?
- Try revising a section of your narrative by using one of the techniques you've just listed. Be sure that you are borrowing the technique only (not the ideas!).
- If the writer has used more than one type of document (more than one *genre*), how are the other documents woven in? What helps the different pieces hang together? Have you considered adding images or other types of texts to your narrative? What will help your text hang together?

Suggested Reading: To learn more about reading like a writer, check out Mike Bunn's essay "How to Read Like a Writer." The complete citation for the essay is on the Works Cited page at the back of this book.

NOTES

VIVID DESCRIPTION

One key element of a good story is vivid description. In other words, writing in a way that helps your audience *see* what you see.

Here's a simple activity to help demonstrate what we mean.

First, think about the place where you spend the most time every day. Is it your dorm room? Maybe it's your apartment? The library?

Now, if you were in that space right now, what would you see?

What sounds would you be likely to hear?

What about smells? What sorts of smells would be in the air?

What about taste? This one might not seem as relevant, but give it a try. Maybe you eat pizza in your dorm room a lot. Describe the taste.

Finally, think about touch. What sorts of things could you touch in that place? Soft, warm bedsheets? The bright blue rug in the center of the floor? The delicately curved keys on your computer keyboard? Write about it.

Great! Now think about doing this activity for each and every place that appears in your narrative. You may not use all of the writing you create from this activity, but the point is that you will have a lot of writing to draw from. You'll just need to make decisions about what information will be most memorable and meaningful for your readers.

NOTES

TENSION AND TURN

Tension and turn are important elements to any good story. Without it, readers are left with narratives that are more like lists than anything else. Did you ever write a "What I Did on My Summer Vacation" essay in which you simply told the audience the activities from your summer vacation—one by one? Let's try to avoid that.

To develop tension in a story, there are several basic things you can do.

First, identify a goal. If you think about the television shows, books, or movies that you enjoy most, you'll probably realize that each one does a good job at creating tension. The main character—or protagonist—has some goal that he or she is trying to reach, whether it's destroying an evil ring, saving the planet, or surviving a zombie apocalypse.

Second, create some doubt. For the tension to really rise, the audience has to wonder whether or not the protagonist is going to achieve her or his goal.

Third, describe the turning point. The turning point is that moment in a story where things reach a climax, allowing the story to move into a resolution and conclusion.

Now, in the space below, try to do this for your own narrative.

1. Identify the goal of the main character—most likely, you.
2. Identify the source of tension in your narrative. Try writing it as a question. For example, "Will Edgar finish his narrative before time runs out?"
3. Identify the turning point where things were "do or die" or "now or never" or when you came to some new realization.

You can even try this out for other narrative ideas. Who knows? You might discover that one story proves to be even more interesting once you think about it.

NOTES

Activity: The Down Draft

The following strategies can help you generate a quick draft that you can use as a starting point. Write quickly for 10 minutes, without planning or organizing—but also without stopping! Write what you remember. If you get stuck, write "I'm stuck here" and go on. If you know what you need to do but can't do it yet, describe it. Try one or more of these activities and see where it leads you.

1. **Three moments.** Choose at least three distinctly separate time periods in your life. Begin each section with "I am ______ years old," and freewrite from there for 10 minutes. (An alternative is to think of three songs or three photographs from distinctly separate times in your life. If you choose this option, start each section with a title or caption.) Stay in the present tense. After reading what you've written, see whether you can find any thematic connections or common images that would link the sections together. You might also consider what happened in the world, in history, during the time of these events and how that might tie into your own history.

2. **Three readers.** Focus on one event. Who would be interested in the event? Who might learn something from your story? Who might give you a new insight? One reader might be a stranger who witnessed the event; another might be a new friend who would understand something about you from your story; yet another might be a much younger or much older person (perhaps a young cousin or a grandparent); another might be a person in authority. No matter who you choose for your three readers, be sure they differ in terms of what each knows about you and what they need to know. Write for about 3 minutes as you tell the same story to each of the readers you have in mind.

   How much background information do you need to give each reader to make the most impact? What language, details, images, or genres change as you tell the story more than once to different types of readers? How might you connect these three accounts? What language, details, or images might recur in all three accounts? (An alternate approach might try three different genres to tell the same story such as a letter, a news release or news article, and a Facebook profile. Again, the challenge is to consider what changes, what stays the same, and what connects the three.)

3. **Flashdraft.** Choose one important life event that has had an impact on your present view of life in general—it might be something you were able to give or teach someone else; some moment when you failed, but moved on; the loss of someone special to you; a lesson you learned or a skill you mastered; an unexpected gift you received; a goal you achieved; or some other surprising circumstance. Write for about 10 minutes. As quickly as possible, describe the moment or event in chronological order first, providing as much detail as you can.

Once you have 2 pages:

- Give your narrative to a reader who will ask questions in the margins. These questions may be journalistic: who, what, when, where, and why? Or they may be sensory: what smells, tastes, sounds, sights, or textures do you associate with this moment or event? Or they may ask for specific details, such as responses, reactions, or dialogue.
- Change to a different color of ink and begin adding answers to your reader's questions, trying to give rich, sensory detail.
- Consider changing the order of the telling. Experiment by beginning the short write in the middle of the story (or the end) and use flashbacks and foreshadowing to help the reader anticipate what happens next.
- Consider different genres you might use to tell your story. How would the different pieces connect?

NOTES

NOTES

UNDERSTANDING FEEDBACK

Interpreting feedback and translating it into specific things to do for your writing can be a challenging aspect of improving as a writer.

- What do you do if your instructor doesn't give you a list of specific things to improve?
- What do you do if you disagree with feedback that your instructor gives you?
- What do you do if the person giving you feedback is a novice writer like you?

To help you navigate this challenging, and sometimes frustrating, part of the writing process, here are a few important principles to keep in mind.

1. **Own Your Writing**. Your writing is just that—yours. You are in charge of what it says and how it says it. That means you need to make decisions about which suggestions you act on and which suggestions you ignore. If your instructor suggests changes that you are uncertain about, you should talk to your instructor. Find out more about why he or she made that suggestion. Explain your own rationale to your instructor. In most cases, a disagreement can lead to a deeper understanding of writing, rhetoric, and conventions.

2. **Collect Multiple Perspectives.** One of the most common concerns when it comes to feedback is knowing when someone is making a good, overall suggestion and when that person is just making a suggestion based on their own preferences or (mis)perceptions about what good writing looks like. To make sure that you're not being led down the wrong path, talk to multiple people and ask specific questions. If four out of five classmates think your introduction is boring, that might be a sign it needs some work. If one person out of ten can't identify your main idea, you can be pretty confident that your main idea is clear.

In the space below, describe the most helpful feedback you ever received on your writing. What did the person say? How did he or she say it?

NOTES

Activity: Peer Review

Read through the essay and, along the way, mark on the essay:

- where you're confused, or where the writing is unclear (~~~ wavy line beneath problematic sentences)
- where writing is strong (✓ check mark next to outstanding sentences)
- where you feel there should be more detail (a plus sign where there should be more)

On a blank sheet of paper, write:

- Name of Writer:
- Name of Reviewer:

Then answer the following questions:

- Did the opening paragraph catch your attention or was there part of it that could be cut? (There often is something that can be cut in rough drafts.)
- What story has the author chosen to tell?
- What were some of the sensory details, description, or imagery that you liked? Where could the writer include more details?
- Does the essay focus in on *a scene or specific moment* from the writer's experiences? Should the story be focused more on one incident/cut down in its scope?
- Why does the writer want to tell this story, and why should the reader want to read it?
- Does the author use multiple genres to tell the story? Should s/he? Why or why not?
- How does the essay's organization (or lack of organization) help or hurt the writer's ability to communicate the central idea? How else might the writer organize the story?
- Does the writer use any clichés or overly sentimental moments? How can these be more unique?
- What suggestions do you have for a catchy title?
- What other suggestions can you provide?

Return the marked-up essay and the answers to these questions to the essay's author.

NOTES

POLISHING YOUR PAPER

Choosing the Right Word

On pages 1–10 of your *Easy Writer* textbook, you'll find a list of the twenty most common errors first-year writers make in their writing. What is interesting is that by far the most common error for first-year writers is choosing the wrong word. As Andrea Lunsford suggests,

> Twenty years ago, spelling errors were most common by a factor of more than three to one. The use of spell checkers has reduced the number of spelling errors in student writing—but spell checkers' suggestions may also be responsible for some (or many) of the wrong words students are using. (1)

That's because the spell checker will suggest a correctly spelled word that sounds like the word the writer is trying to use, even though the spell check suggestion has a different meaning.

Here are a few words and phrases to watch out for:

- manner vs. manor
- for all intents and purposes vs. for all intensive purposes
- definitely vs. defiantly
- credible vs. creditable
- there vs. their vs. they're
- its vs. it's
- let's vs. lets
- then vs. than
- possess vs. posses
- manager vs. manger
- customer vs. costumer

Here's a two-step method for reducing and eliminating these mistakes in your writing.

Step 1: Read your paper out loud *slowly*. Reading slowly is important because the sound may help you identify things that are working and things that aren't working.

Step 2: Make a list. Write down any words or phrases that are not correct as well as their corrections. You can also write down any words that you want to double check, just to make sure you're using them correctly. Use this page to start your list.

NOTES

SAMPLE NARRATIVE

Zachary Droppa

Droppa 1

ENGL 101-036

4/26/12

Awe-Filled/Dreamer

Journal 1/22/12

I have always been a dreamer; I have always imagined things much grander and more complex and important than myself. In my childhood, I pretended that my sheep's pasture was a fantastic realm, where I was neither the strongest nor the hero, but I was simply a visitor learning of the complex and powerful beings of my world. I have read a large number of books and played a large number of text-based games in which I imagined the gorgeous, vast worlds that the author created, wishing to be able to be inside the worlds myself. Finally, I found my love, mathematics, which is the ultimate magical mystery. The following are a few hypotheses or possible contributing factors as to why I am this way.

My favourite toy as a child was a clear plastic dome with a button on top which, when pushed, would make coloured balls bounce around and land in cups, and I would try to predict how certain balls would get in certain combinations of cups. My mother would read to me not just children's fairy tales, but fantasy books by Anne McCaffrey and J. R. R. Tolkien. Later, in my AP Statistics class, I was constantly reminded of that childish wonder of probability and mathematics. In my teens, I read science fiction that displayed the fantastically unknown and exciting expanse of space and wonderful possibilities of the future of humanity. Perhaps these things allude to a developmental attachment to the imaginary and abstract.

My mother has probably been the largest influence on me in just about every possible way. I have always considered her a form of magic; the way she can succeed

NOTES

at almost anything she does, and stay resolutely optimistic however bad things get absolutely amazes me. In particular, the way she stood up to my father's attitude astonished me and helped plant and nurture that belief of her heroic nature. One of our favourite authors, Terry Pratchett, describes his witches similarly to how I see my mother: sharp-witted, with their head above everyone else's—all the way up in the sky. A lot of who I am is just me trying to dream as big as she does.

No matter who tried to hold me back, I've always tried to push upwards. Whether this wonder of the unknown is due to my mother's influence or my own experiences, I enjoy who I am.

In Which I Give a Speech on Maths to High School Students

My high school sent an e-mail to their alumni near the end of the fall semester, asking us to talk to juniors and seniors about how great college is or whatever, and shortly afterwards my former maths teacher, Mrs. Ritenour, sent me an e-mail asking if I would like to be a guest speaker for their Maths Club. Maths is one of those topics for me that excites and amazes me, that fills me with a feeling of the greatest awe, so I replied with an enthusiastic, "I would love to!"

With no idea what topic to give a presentation on, I attempted to make a list of all of the things that I have enough interest in to give a speech about: Induction, Fields, Cardinality, Combinatorics, Modular Arithmetic. . . there was too much! I then decided to focus on subjects that both I knew enough about and that would be able to hold the attention of high school students, and I was able to narrow it down to two subjects: Cardinality and Knot Theory. I ended up picking Knot Theory because it was more fun, more visual, and there were YouTube videos I liked that were related to it, even though I knew significantly less about it. I didn't want to give my

NOTES

presentation on something with a whole lot of equations to bore them; I wanted to show them the mystery and awe of the unknown, albeit perhaps impractical.

I decided I was going to try the same method of teaching that my teacher used to teach to me. I didn't want to plan too much and make it seem rote, but I worried more that it would not be planned enough. I decided they would need a two-ish minute intro to modular arithmetic in order to get the one equation I would present, and then I could get to the meat of the material. Eventually I convinced myself to relax, as it isn't a horribly complex subject.

The day came to guest-speak for the math club, and I decided to get there nice and early; I arrived an hour before school started, right as Mrs. Ritenour did. Finding a comfortable location for my bag, I took out my notes and placed them up front, taking a seat at the table behind which Mrs. Ritenour would teach. I started to space out, imagining the speech to come, preparing and recalling my notes. Mrs. Ritenour started, "School doesn't start for another hour . . ."

Regaining my bearings, I replied, "Oh, yeah, I know, I . . . I guess I'll go talk to friends."

I spent the next hour walking around, greeting old friends and trying to gather a congregation to maths club. I eventually returned to the maths room and waited for the club to arrive. The room full, I realized maths club seemed to have grown since I was in it. Even the former head of the school's math department, Mr. Snyder, was there. I would like to say I wasn't nervous, but I felt a responsibility to try to convey the sense of wonder that maths gives me to those in maths club. They gave a reminder to brainstorm designs for their Pi Day shirts, which always end up being done just barely in time, and the floor was mine.

NOTES

Droppa 4

I started on the modular arithmetic vocabulary, deciding not to write them down due to my block of time only being about 20 minutes and me having terrible handwriting. I got to the knots, drawing a few knots, realizing I had forgotten the exact definition of them. Nevertheless, I spat out a fairly accurate definition of knots, explained the significance of the unknot, or the knot that is not a knot, and moved on to the Reidemeister moves. I almost ran out of room writing them down, slightly confusing the order. I ended with the concept of 3-colourability and p-colourability, writing the equation for crossings down. I then realized that this uses notation of modular arithmetic, which I had neglected to write. I hastily explained the symbols, finished p-colourability, and asked, "How much do you think you understand? Two percent? Three?"

I got an optimistic, "Twenty or thirty!" from near the front, and various murmurs from the back. I answered a couple questions about colourability, and once all questions were answered, I started the YouTube video I mentioned earlier related to knots. Just as the video finished, the bell rang, and all of the students ran off to their next class. Mrs. Ritenour beamed at me, stating I had excelled, and that my love of mathematics really came through; I humbly replied that it wasn't a very good presentation. I left the room unsure of how I'd done. A few days later, I received an e-mail from Mr. Snyder stating that he had enjoyed my presentation, but don't think my presentation was successful unless I transmitted a little bit of the awe I feel for mathematics to some of the students there.

Panspermia

If I could wish upon a star

I'd wish to voyage on an Ark

a seed of life, a one-way trip

NOTES

into the stars; another world

disperse our eggs in many nests

let aeons pass to find our world

a world anew in which to grow

an independent human race

our ancestors left far away

above, within the heavens new

one lone star, Sol, may soon become

the birthplace of a legacy

the thoughts I think one starry night

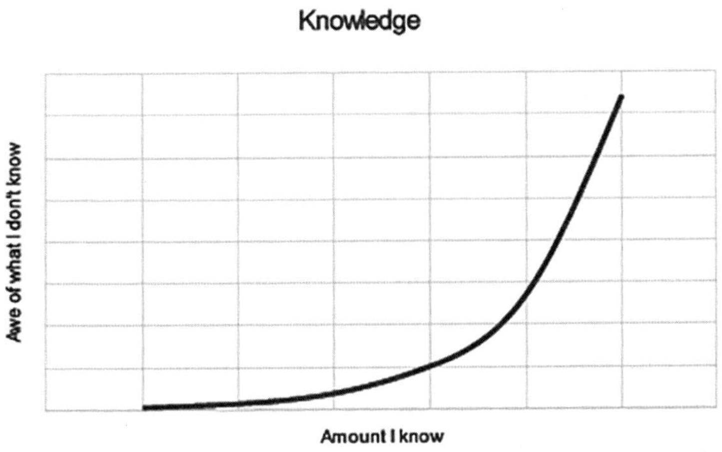

NOTES

The Future: A Stream of Consciousness

Sitting at my computer, there is a slight ache in my left arm. Looking down, I recall an article I read once: "Scrapheap Transhumanism," remembering its advice. It stated that Transhumanists, or people who believe technology is a sort of means of accelerating evolution, should start augmenting their bodies *now*. I turn my hand around to look at my fingers, feeling the tips of each. They talked about how one could place a magnetic sensor in one's finger, so whenever one was near a strong power line, one's finger would buzz. They also said things about placing RFID tags in wrists, but now I am thinking about a speech that I watched Kurt Vonnegut give about his being a Luddite, that is, one who believes technology is inherently bad for humanity. He argued that it was making us lazier and more stupid. A quizzical frown crosses my face; I disagree vehemently. Neuroscience demonstrates that when one picks up an item, such as a baseball bat or my pencil, the brain recognises that object as part of your body. I pick up said pencil and twirl it in my hand. The brain actually thinks pencils are a sort of hand add-on, or app, that is not significantly different from having a piece of graphite physically attached to your finger. The implications! Imagine when the first brain did this: perhaps *Homo erectus* was the first cyborg!

My mind drifts off; I look to the sun casting light on the far wall. I think of lights spreading from a ceiling to a wall, that light hitting the wall in an imperfect hyperbola. Math is everywhere, man. Periodic movement of the tree outside my window, how crowds such as the loud one walking past move, how a chain or rope falls held at two points, how soap bubbles form between two parallel circles . . . I need another Rolo. Today was tough, what with the fire alarm at 4 A.M. and the PRT being broken, preventing me from writing this very paper, but I have to continue; this is no excuse to take it easy. I have big plans: I want to graduate in three (or 3.5) years.

NOTES

Droppa 7

I want to get into one of the best maths graduate programs (I need to look up where to apply). I want to get a doctorate in maths. (or maybe something else entirely) (or maybe I won't finish my graduate studies, maybe an Opportunity will come along) (maybe I will become less interested in maths once I get my B.S., and will study psychology or computer engineering or . . .) (or maybe the need to stay near Valerie, my love, will complicate things further) I realize fully that a "complete person" is a silly concept; I am constantly changing from the Yesterday Me to the Today Me (who is kind of a dick due to my strict sleep schedule being messed up) to the Tomorrow Me. (who hopefully has everything all figured out) (some people say I have everything figured out. I laugh to myself.)

NOTES

2

Reflective Cover Memo

Date: ______________________________

To (Instructor's Name): ______________________________

From (Author of Paper): ______________________________

Subject: ______________________________

Reflective Cover Memo for "Final for Now"—Multi-Angle Personal Narrative

Writing Process. Please reflect on your writing process. What did you try for the first time? What comments from peer workshop and conferences did you explore in your revision? How did this improve your paper? Please describe concrete examples.

____

____

____

____

____

____

Trouble Spots. What did you find most challenging about this project? How did you deal with these challenges? What did you learn from composing this project?

____

____

____

____

____

____

Future Writing. What plans do you have for revisions of this paper for the Final Portfolio draft? For instance, what else might you have discussed if you had more time/space? What would you do differently?

____

____

____

____

____

____

Questions or Comments. What questions do you have for me about the construction of your paper or the writing process? What would you like me to focus on while I read the "Final for Now" version of this paper?

CHAPTER 3

Writing to Tell Someone Else's Story

This project asks you to move from writing about yourself to writing about someone (or something) else.

GETTING STARTED

Overview of Project: Writing to Tell Someone Else's Story

PURPOSE

The purpose of this assignment is to build on what you've learned about description and organization while changing perspective. Instead of telling your own story, you now have to tell someone (or something) else's story. Here are a few additional goals for this chapter:

- Recognize and analyze the ethical issues involved in representing others.
- Conduct primary research in the form of an interview.
- Conduct secondary research in order to understand your subject's context.
- Integrate other voices into your writing—through summary, paraphrase, and quotation.

GENRE

One common genre for this type of writing is the profile. Typically, profiles provide an in-depth description of a person, place, organization, or event. They help a reader see the profile's subject in a more complex way, often uncovering elements of the subject that are unexpected or unique. For example, a profile of a famous movie star might describe how the person is "down to earth" or supports several humanitarian causes.

AUDIENCE

Your instructor may have specific instructions about what audience to write for. Otherwise, consider what sort of newspaper, magazine, or website would likely publish a profile on your topic. Do some critical thinking and research to help you imagine that audience.

NOTES

ORGANIZATION

Like narratives, there are many ways a profile might be organized. Listen for your instructor to give you specific instructions about how to organize your story. One thing to avoid, however, is turning in an interview transcript. Your profile should sound more like your narrative and less like a back and forth discussion where you write the question and then write the person's answer. A transcript can be a useful tool for your profile, but you shouldn't turn it in as your actual profile.

ASSESSMENT

Your instructor may adjust the criteria below to fit the specific project for your course. In any case, here are a few key criteria to keep in mind:

- Propose a strong and appropriate topic
- Find an appropriate interview subject
- Use description to fully contextualize your subject
- Introduce quoted material smoothly and correctly
- Use and engage an audience-appropriate tone of voice
- Document any sources (including your interview) ethically and accurately through in-text citations and a Works Cited list (using guidelines found in *Easy Writer*)
- Produce approximately 1,200 to 1,500 words (4–5 pages) of polished writing

TURNING IT IN

The assignment is due: ____________________

I need to ____

____

____

NOTES

MIND MAPPING

Do you remember in Chapter 2 when we mentioned that invention was the name we give to activities that help us come up with ideas? Freewriting was the example in the last chapter. In this chapter, we're going to introduce you to mind mapping, which you're probably already familiar with. This activity is also frequently called clustering, or simply, brainstorming.

It's a straightforward activity. You simply write a word in the middle of a sheet of paper and then add words and ideas that relate to it. In the example below, we've focused on the start of a mind map that might help you choose a focus for your profile. We've even left a few of the boxes blank so that you can write in your own ideas.

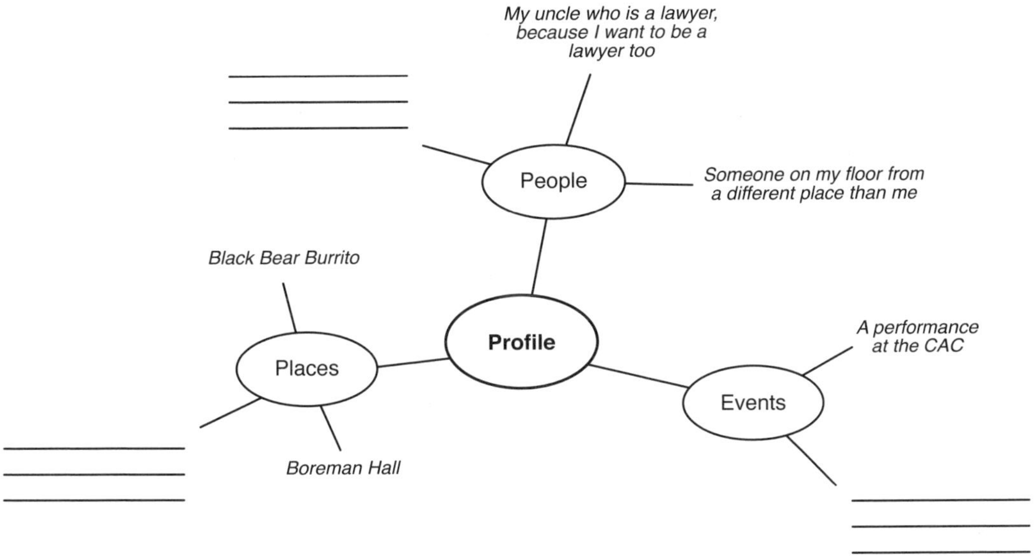

Great! Now why don't you take a few minutes to create a mind map of your own? You can choose anything. If you're having trouble coming up with something, try making a mind map of interesting places at WVU.

NOTES

Activity: Writing a Lead

The first paragraph always has to do a lot of work: it must grab the reader's interest, provide enough context to tell the reader what he or she will be reading about, and encourage the reader to continue reading.

Writers often call this beginning a "lead." The goal in writing a strong lead is to convince a casual reader to stop scanning and actually read the whole article. This is the reason it needs to be interesting. A strong lead should do the following:

- Capture the readers' imaginations by raising questions.
- Contain some essence of the story. Readers should have some sense of what the story is about and why they should care.
- Set the mood and tone—is this going to be a funny story, tragic, hard-hitting, or celebratory?
- Be as concise as possible. In other words, it should cover all these points quickly and powerfully.

The good news is that the lead doesn't have to be the first thing you write. Try a few different leads—and be sure to get some feedback—before you settle on the right one.

TYPES OF LEADS

Try writing one version of each type of lead as you think about the introduction for your own feature article.

Summary Lead: Summarizes the most important/newsworthy elements in the story (typically in one sentence)—the Who, What, Where, and When. It is also known as the standard lead, and is the most common.

Single-Item Lead: Concentrates on just one or two of the 5 Ws for a bigger punch.

NOTES

Cartridge Lead: Uses one word or a short phrase as a teaser for the rest of the lead. Often, this can seem gimmicky, and this tactic should be used artfully and sparingly, if at all.

Question Lead: Poses a question to the reader, which the story proceeds to answer. This can also seem gimmicky and should be used sparingly. If used, it needs to be followed up by the necessary contextual information.

Anecdotal Lead: Makes use of story and description to draw the reader in.

NOTES

Activity: Reading Like a Writer—Profile

For this activity you will read a sample profile and answer a few questions about it. We have included a sample student profile after this worksheet to help you, or your instructor may ask you to read a different example.

Title of Article: ______________________________

Author: ______________________________

Source: ______________________________

Purpose. What is the author trying to accomplish with this article? How do you know? List details from the article that help you to understand the purpose.

____

____

____

____

____

____

Audience. Who you think this profile is written for? Be as specific as you can in terms of age, gender, occupation, and characteristics like that.

____

____

____

____

____

____

Conventions. What sorts of conventions do you notice in terms of things like formatting or content?

____

____

____

____

____

____

____

What about the lead? Explain how the article tries to "hook" your interest.

NOTES

What about how the profile ends? Explain how the author brings the article to a conclusion.

NOTES

SAMPLE PROFILE

Aaron Neely

Neely 1

Nital Shippy

101.11

3 Oct. 2011

Behind the PRT

Friday September 23, 2011. I approach the Beechurst Personal Rapid Transit station on my way to my interview. I have scheduled to meet with Arlie Forman, associate director of the PRT, at his office in the main maintenance shop at the bottom of 8th street. To get there, I have been instructed to arrange a special ride on the PRT. My first objective: locate the station telephone.

I find the phone in a black box next the elevator on the ground level below the platforms. A few seconds after picking up the phone I hear the voice of the operator:

"Operator."

"Yes, hello, I have a meeting with Mr. Forman. He told me to speak with you to have a car sent for me to bring me to the, uh, maintenance center . . . ?"

"All right, hang on . . . OK, vehicle 46. I'll call the elevator for you."

Sure enough, the elevator doors next to me open, seemingly of their own accord. I ride the elevator up and walk out onto the platform. As I near vehicle 46, its door opens as if it had been patiently awaiting my arrival. Once the operator has told all other passengers to exit the car, the door shuts, and the car takes me out of the station. It is quickly diverted from the normal path and taken down to the maintenance building. When the car finally comes to a stop, several PRT employees are waiting for me outside the building.

NOTES

Neely 2

If the Big Brother-esque monitoring and control of the PRT system had not already impressed me, the maintenance shop certainly would have. I am led through a massive garage door and between two vehicles with missing panels toward several more at the back of the shop that are raised 10′ into the air on large lifts. Miscellaneous parts and tools are strewn about the shop. Mr. Forman is speaking with several of the maintenance men as I approach. It is obvious he runs a very tight ship; everyone is focused and on task-solving problems. After I introduce myself, he leads me up a set of stairs into a break room and then up another and down a hall to his office. The sharp contrast between workshop and office space reminds me of a factory or industrial plant. We sit down to talk; I don't really know what to expect from this interview. Within 10 minutes, I have been completely blown away by the sheer volume of new information Forman is sharing with me. The first thing I find out? The Morgantown PRT system was originally an experiment.

The personal rapid transit (PRT) system concept had long been considered a viable solution for severe urban congestion and had even gained the interest of President Richard Nixon. The hilly terrain, student need for transportation, and far-spread campuses made Morgantown the perfect test subject for this kind of system, so the federal government paid Boeing Aerospace $62 million for the initial construction (Walnut, Beechurst, and Engineering) and then later an additional $64 million for an expansion (Towers and Medical) (Forman).The system was originally designed to have a 20-year lifespan. This is its 37th. This extreme age has brought about many serious problems, most of which are becoming increasingly difficult and costly to manage. One of the main issues the PRT faces today is scarcity of parts. The vehicles of the PRT system were custom built nearly forty years ago; the parts used in its construction were made by companies and suppliers that either no longer make

NOTES

the parts or are no longer in business. This means that most replacement parts must be custom fabricated, a process that is extremely expensive. To make matters worse, Boeing used many aircraft components in the construction of the vehicles. There are two problems with this choice. First, replacing these higher-grade components is complicated and costly. Second, many of these parts are impractical for use beyond testing in their current application. For example, the cylinders behind the bumpers on the vehicles that absorb the force of impact in the event of a collision permanently compress after only one use. Crews must then replace the entire part to make the vehicle safe again (Forman). Mr. Forman's reaction to this design choice paralleled my own. As he put it, "Why would you do that? The only thing I can think of is you just had a lot of them around."

There are many other problems with the PRT's age and design that cause problems on a daily basis. For example, the onboard computers used by the vehicles are still the original analog units the system was originally built with. The primary train control computer system has recently been updated to newer host PCs, but it still carries a directly translated version of the buggy program written for it back in the 70's. Because neither of these pieces of 70's tech has been produced for some time, there is no technical support available for them. If there are any problems, the PRT maintenance crew must figure out solutions on their own (Forman).

As if these issues weren't complicated enough, the PRT faces the problem of having a limited number of working vehicles. Mr. Forman told me, "To leave it in automatic mode . . . we would need 55 vehicles, probably, working out on the guideway. Today, we have 38 that are worthy of operation." This means that, of the original 71 vehicles in operation at the opening of the PRT, nearly half are currently unusable. This truly is a sad state of affairs.

NOTES

Neely 4

Currently, the largest concern for the people in charge of keeping the PRT up and running is managing cost. As they begin to replace the aircraft-grade parts with automotive-based substitutes, the expense of repairs will hopefully decline.

In addition to general design updates, the engineers of the PRT are working on a new onboard computer for the vehicles. These new computers will be completely digital and will be able to communicate with the stations and control centers through a series of wireless transmitters and receivers spaced throughout the track.

Finally, the engineers are also planning to replace the drive system the vehicles currently use with a new, updated design. Unfortunately, these improvements will require money the PRT just doesn't have at the moment. Still, Mr. Forman told me that if all of the proposed improvements were made, approximately 65% of the downtime events they experience now would be resolved.

As I speak with Mr. Forman about these problems, I can clearly hear the frustration in his voice. I can tell he genuinely cares about the PRT system and the students who rely on it. He makes no excuses for the downtime that plagues the system, but instead completely accepts the great need for improvement. He tells me he is not alone in this; that the rest of the team in charge of the PRT's operation is as devoted to finding solutions as he is.

By the end of our exchange, I honestly feel sympathy for Mr. Forman and the rest of the PRT crew's plight. These people fight tooth and nail every day to pull this dying machine back from the brink of a total shutdown, and do so while receiving virtually constant criticism.

NOTES

People in the Morgantown community and WVU students are very quick to complain about the PRT, but they seldom consider where they would be without it. With the buses overwhelmed if it is down for more than 20 minutes; what would happen if the PRT shut down altogether? I think what is needed here is a call to action. Whether they realize it or not, thousands of people depend on the PRT every day. The community needs to band together to support fixing some of these problems and keeping the PRT alive. At this point, the biggest issue is funding, so perhaps a group of students could convince the University to allocate extra funds to the PRT for the much-needed repairs. Maybe Engineering students could be placed in internships to gain hands-on experience by working on the PRT while expanding its labor force.

No matter what the answer is, something must be done, and soon. The PRT is on its last legs, and I, for one, do not care to think about the nightmarish commute we will all face if we allow it to complete its slow descent into a rusty death.

NOTES

Works Cited

Forman, Arlie. Personal Interview. 23 Sept. 2011

Works Referenced

Alter, Lloyd. "Richard Nixon Proves Personal Transit Actually Can Work." *Treehugger*. Discovery Communications, 12 June 2007. Web. 28 Sept. 2011.

NOTES

HOW TO USE INTERVIEW TRANSCRIPTS

After you complete an interview, it will be helpful to transcribe the questions and the answers into a document so that you can use the interview as source material for your profile. You might use the interview material in several ways.

1. **Direct Quoting:** Turn your transcript over so you can't see it. Attempt to recall, from memory, any direct quotes that were particularly striking. If possible, list them on the back of your transcript or a separate sheet of paper. Afterward, check your transcript and see what else you may want to directly quote and mark the passages.

2. **Paraphrase and Summary:** Next, using your transcript, go through and decide what you may want to paraphrase or summarize. Remember that paraphrasing typically involves taking all the main points and rewording the ideas yourself. Look for the places in your interview that would be best served by this method. On your transcript, mark each passage in a way that makes sense to you. Remember it is almost certain that you won't use every aspect of your interview, and that's okay.

3. **Finding an Angle:** Sometimes after you conduct an interview, you start to see what's commonly called an *angle.*

   Think of angle this way: Your topic is the subject—person, place, event, organization—that you're writing about, but your angle is the specific focus that makes your topic the most interesting to an audience. Often the best angles challenge preconceptions that audiences have for a subject.

   For example, one WVU student chose to write about the school's rifle team (topic). The student then focused the story on the perspective of the only female member of the team (angle).

3

Workshop: Peer Review for the Profile

Author:____

Title: ____

Reader:____

In this workshop, **you will be a magazine editor.** You will work in groups to do the kind of roundtable editing/responding that real publishers and editors do all the time. Your group will be given papers belonging to other students in the class (you will not read your group members' papers), and you will read them and respond to them, imagining that you are the editors addressed in the cover letters, committed to publishing these feature articles in your magazine. What does the writer still need to do to grab and keep the audience's attention? How is the author's research? How well has the author cited sources? Is the author's interview in-depth and engaging? Does the author use exciting, vivid description to bring the person, place, or event to life for the reader?

Step One: You should be in groups of two to four for this workshop, though no group will be given more than three papers to read. Begin by physically moving so you can easily talk to all your group members. Introduce yourselves. Now each of you pick up a paper and begin reading. Read the whole paper without marking on it. Then make a few notes in the space provided for "Reader 1." When you are done, pass the paper and the comment sheet to a group member and proceed to the next paper, reading and making notes until everyone in the group has read all the papers.

Step Two: Discuss the papers, assigning one person to take notes in the space provided for "Group Feedback." Go through the papers in any order you like, responding to the concerns suggested. Also feel free to add any suggestions or points of praise that your group feels are warranted. And if the group members disagree, note that too (e.g., *Some of us thought your interview was a bit short and lacked depth, but other members of the group thought it was sufficient*).

Here are the things to make notes on for each paper:

- How well does the introduction grab your attention? How could it be improved?
- Does the writer use vivid, exciting language throughout? Is something particularly well evoked or missing (e.g., a description of a person or place)?
- How well does the interview (or interviews) work here? Is it Q&A format, are quotes poorly incorporated or not memorable, is there enough interview material?
- Is their research incorporated? Cited? Could it be done more smoothly? Is there background information missing that you wish was included?
- Does this article KEEP your attention all the way to the end? How? How could it be made more engaging?

Paper Title: ______________________________ **Author:** ______________________

Reader 1

Reader 2

Reader 3

Group Feedback

3 Reflective Cover Memo

Date: ______________________________

To (Instructor's Name): ______________________________

From (Author of Paper): ______________________________

Subject: ______________________________

Reflective Cover Memo for "Final for Now"—Feature Article

Writing Process. Please reflect on your writing process. What did you try for the first time? What comments from peer workshop and conferences did you explore in your revision? How did this improve your paper? Please describe concrete examples.

____

____

____

____

____

____

Trouble Spots. What questions do you wish you had asked—what could have been done differently? What did you find most challenging about this project—and how did you deal with those challenges?

____

____

____

____

____

____

Purpose. How did you decide the focus of your article? What was your focus? What quotes and observations did you use to focus your article? How did you do this? Talk about how you handled quotes and details effectively and where this may have been difficult.

____

____

____

____

____

____

Future Writing. What plans do you have for revisions of this paper for the final portfolio draft? What else might you have discussed in the feature article if you had more time/space?

Questions or Comments. What questions do you have for me about the construction of your paper or the writing process? What would you like me to focus on while I read the "Final for Now" version of this paper?

NOTES

POLISHING YOUR PAPER

Introductory Elements

The second most common mistake among first-year writers is a missing comma after introductory elements. An introductory element is "any word, phrase, or clause that precedes the subject of a sentence" (Lunsford 110). Here is an example:

To pass the course, students must attend class and spend time studying.

Here are a few words and phrases that might help you identify introductory elements:

Before	(Before going to class, you need to . . .)
After	(After I got home, I . . .)
However	(However, I feel that . . .)
Although	(Although the topic was boring, the speaker . . .)
As	(As time went by, I began to realize . . .)
On the other hand	(On the other hand, I like . . .)

Here are two strategies for identifying introductory elements in your writing:

1. **Strategy #1: On the Computer.** Use the search feature in your word processor to search for each of the phrases above. Read each example one-by-one and decide whether you have an introductory element that needs a comma.
2. **Strategy #2: On Paper**. Scan your paper for each of these words and phrases. When you find one, highlight it. When you finish scanning for each, go back and decide whether or not you need to add a comma.

Just for fun, record all of the introductory elements you find in your paper on this page and count how many times you use each one. You might start to see a pattern, which will give you an opportunity to talk to your instructor about style and sentence variation.

For more on commas with introductory elements, see section 19a in *Easy Writer*.

CHAPTER 4 Writing to Reflect

In this chapter, we take stock of what we've covered so far and practice for the final portfolio.

GETTING STARTED

Overview of Project: Writing to Reflect

PURPOSE

There are two purposes for this assignment. The first is to give you an opportunity to think through what you've already learned in this course. You want to have some idea of where you've been, so you can think more clearly about where you're going. Reflection will help you uncover the things you know and identify things to work on.

The second purpose is to give you practice at compiling your portfolio before the final portfolio at the end of the course. Your final portfolio—where you show your instructor everything you've learned—will determine a large portion of your grade (70%). Therefore, it's important for you to practice putting it together now so that you can identify any trouble spots and get rid of them before it's time to get graded.

GENRE

The genre that we're going to focus on in this chapter is the memo. Memos are common documents in professional workplaces. They have a very specific format, and they are often direct. In other words, they get right to the point.

AUDIENCE

Your instructor may have specific instructions about what audience to write for, but in general, you should speak directly to your instructor.

NOTES

ORGANIZATION

While your instructor may give you specific instructions about how to organize your memo, you can also consult several online resources to help you get the general idea. One great online resource is the Purdue OWL (https://owl.english.purdue.edu/owl/). If you go to that website and search for "memos," you'll find many resources. Another online resource is WVU's SpeakWrite website (https://speakwrite.wvu.edu/student-resources).

ASSESSMENT

All English 101 courses have the same core criteria for assessing portfolios. There are two places in this book where you can look for portfolio assessment criteria. The first is on the back inside cover of this book. This is really more of a checklist to help you think about and reflect on the course goals. The second place is the rubric on page 2 that describes what superior portfolios look like, what strong portfolios look like, what satisfactory portfolios look like, and so on.

TURNING IT IN

The assignment is due: ________________

I need to ____

____

____

NOTES

MIDTERM REFLECTION

Date: ____

To: English 101 Class Members

From: English 101 Professor

Subject: Writer's Reflection at Midterm

Your ongoing project in English 101 is to develop your abilities as an effective reader, researcher, and writer. I ask you to take stock of your progress in the class at midterm point and again at the end of the semester as you submit your portfolio. Your reflection should take the form of a memo (about 3 pages long). This memo gives you a chance to do three things:

1. Consider your work as a writer, reader, and thinker.
2. Identify some personal writing goals for the remainder of the course (or beyond English 101).
3. Engage in a dialogue with me.

Please use *specific examples* from your work this semester to explain and illustrate your work as a writer, reader, researcher, and thinker. To develop your points, think about what you've accomplished in your exploratory writing, your essays, your responses to group members, and your responses to readings. For additional ideas, you might try reviewing the readings for the class, the syllabus and assignment sheets, and the comments you've received from me and your peers. We'll spend some time in class generating ideas and discussing organization.

Drafting the Memo

The midterm memo should be about 3 pages long. As you draft, think about how you will organize information for me:

- What are the most important points/purposes that you want to convey?
- What specific details will make your points both convincing and interesting?
- How might *headings* help you group information and highlight key points?
- How can you use the memo format, paragraph breaks, bullets, verbal cues, and white space to help guide my reading?
- Is your grammar, spelling, and punctuation under control? How about tone and style?

Keep in mind that the memo itself is another example of your writing. You will have a chance to work on it in class and to get feedback from your peers.

Memo Genre. I am specifically asking you to write in the memo genre to encourage you to think about the relationships among form, audience, and content as you write. This assignment sheet (set up as a memo) offers you one example of some format and layout conventions; note the use of headings and bullets, the spacing, etc. How does the memo format convey/shape the message and address audience in specific ways? How does a memo differ from an essay?

NOTES

Activity: Midterm Assessment of English 101

Instructor Name: ______________________ **Semester/Year:** ______________________

I value your feedback on English 101. This course should be helping you develop and sharpen your writing abilities. I hope you will take a moment at this midterm point to give me your comments and ideas for meeting this goal.

Please respond to the following questions. You may remain anonymous if you like.

1. Which assignments and activities have been most helpful, informative, or useful for you? Please explain why.

2. Would you change any assignment or activity? Please explain why and suggest an improvement or alternative.

3. Are there any aspects of writing that you would like to learn more about?

4. How helpful are class periods, handouts, comments on rough drafts, conferences, and e-mail? Please explain.

5. I welcome any additional comments or suggestions for improvement.

Please use the space below or additional paper if you need more space.
Thanks for taking the time to give me your response.

CHAPTER 5
Writing to Analyze

Chapter 5 builds on what you've learned so far by taking a close look at analysis. That is, dividing something into its parts and explaining how those parts work together.

GETTING STARTED

Overview of Project: Writing to Analyze

PURPOSE

The purpose of this assignment is to practice what you've learned so far about rhetoric and apply it through analysis. You'll notice that we're making a shift here from writing stories about ourselves and people or places nearby. Now we're writing a different kind of story. These stories will ask you to use what you've learned about description, context, and rhetoric to analyze something—in other words, to describe its parts and how those parts all work together. Another way to put it is to say that now you're going to tell a story about what something means.

GENRE

The genre for this chapter is rhetorical analysis. In her essay "Backpacks vs. Briefcases: Steps Toward Rhetorical Analysis," Laura Bolin Carroll suggests that "understanding rhetorical messages is essential to help us to become informed consumers, but it also helps evaluate the ethics of messages, how they affect us personally, and how they affect society" (46). The critical thinking involved in this analysis helps us take steps toward understanding how and why information and messages affect us—whether that information is an advertisement, an e-mail, a movie, or a story.

NOTES

AUDIENCE

Your instructor may have specific instructions about what audience to write for. Otherwise, consider writing for an audience like a family member or a friend. How would you explain rhetoric to that person? How would you explain how the thing you're analyzing works rhetorically?

ORGANIZATION

Listen for your instructor to give you specific instructions about how to organize your rhetorical analysis. In general, you can expect to use an MLA format (see the sample paper in section 41e of *Easy Writer*). You can also expect to include elements like an introduction, a conclusion, a works cited page, and a thesis statement. Finally, you can expect that the body of your paper will do things like explain the context for what you are analyzing, describe what you are analyzing, and discuss how the thing you are analyzing uses rhetoric.

Hint: Worry less about evaluating what you're analyzing and focus more on how it's supposed to work. For example, if you are analyzing an advertisement, don't spend a lot of time (or any time) telling your audience it's a great/awful advertisement. Spend your time explaining how it tries to use things like emotions or logic to persuade an audience.

ASSESSMENT

Your instructor may adjust the criteria below to fit the specific project for your course. In any case, here are a few key criteria to keep in mind:

- Write a thesis focused on the *rhetoric* of the text rather than the topic (*how* and *why* the text works—or fails to work—rather than a statement that simply says what the text is about)
- Find information that helps to contextualize what you're analyzing or supports your ideas about how the thing works. (Hint: Your textbook or *Easy Writer* might be good sources to cite for this project because they describe rhetoric.)
- Organize your paper in a way that helps your reader understand what you analyzed and how it works
- Use well-developed examples, details, and facts based on close analysis
- Conclude your paper by using the strategies described in section 3e of *Easy Writer*
- Format your paper according to MLA guidelines
- Produce approximately 1,200 to 1,500 words (4–5 pages) of polished writing

TURNING IT IN

The assignment is due: ____________________

I need to ____

____

____

Activity: Exploring and Analyzing Texts

NOTES

Analyzing Audience. Read words and images closely for a rhetorical analysis that focuses on audience issues.

- Compare *Elle* and *GQ*. As you look at the content and the ads, who is the target audience for each? How can you tell? What specific examples or details can you point to as evidence? How could you create a thesis statement based on your observations and evidence?
- Compare two cartoons, such as *Family Guy* and *Boondocks*. As you look at the content and the characters (and perhaps the ads that run during the show), who is the target audience for each? How can you tell? What specific examples or details can you point to as evidence? How could you create a thesis statement based on your observations and evidence?
- Look closely at Dave Chappelle's "Wayne Brady" skit. Who is the target audience? How can you tell? What specific examples or details can you point to as evidence? How could you create a thesis statement based on your observations and evidence?

Analyzing Purpose. Read words and images closely for a rhetorical analysis that focuses on purpose as much as audience.

- In the *Batman* movies, compare Jack Nicholson's Joker and Heath Ledger's Joker—two different actors, two different directors, and two very different interpretations. What differs and why? What sort of thesis statement can you create? What evidence do you have (or would you need to research) to support your thesis?
- Choose a Disney film that you know well (e.g., *Cinderella*, *Mulan*, *Beauty and the Beast*). What are some of the key characteristics of the film? What ideas or messages are being presented? How? What evidence do you have (or would you need to research) to support your thesis?

Analyzing Historical Relevance. Read words and images closely for a rhetorical analysis that focuses on historical relevance.

- Watch a music video that uses historical footage (such as System of a Down's "Hypnotize" with its reference to Tiananmen Square). Find five pieces of factual information about that historical context. Discuss how the video's footage manages to (or fails to) relate to the song. Start with a two-sentence summary of the video. Follow the summary with a working thesis statement. What points do you want to make? How will factual information help you develop your points?
- Choose a music video with historical relevance, such as "We Are the World" (recorded by USA for Africa in 1985) or "What's Going On?" (originally recorded by Marvin Gaye in 1971 as an anti-war protest; recorded again in 2001 by Artists against AIDS). Find five pieces of factual information about the historical context. Discuss how the words and images work together to make a statement that is relevant to this particular moment in history. Start with a two-sentence summary of the video. Follow the summary with a working thesis statement. What points do you want to make? How will your factual information help you develop your points?

NOTES

Activity: Searching in Lexis Nexis

For your rhetorical analysis essay, it is important to try and understand how your text was received and written about at the time that it was delivered or released. You should try and do a search that allows you to read newspaper stories about your text in the time immediately after an audience first encountered it. This activity shows you how to perform this research through the WVU Libraries LibGuides page for 101 students.

The **WVU Library website is located at** *lib.wvu.edu.*

- From the home page, click on the tab labeled **Databases**.
- Then type the word **Lexis**.
- On the next screen, select **Lexis Nexis Academic**.
- Enter your keywords in the search box.
- Click **Search**.

You should now be able to read articles about the book, reviews of the book, and other content related to the book from this exact time period. The articles will be listed in order, from most recent to oldest. You should scroll through and try to find the oldest articles, because these are most likely to be direct reactions to the release of the book.

NOTES

WRITING A THESIS STATEMENT

A thesis is a statement that clearly explains an author's main idea for a piece of writing (Lunsford 371). Thesis statements are actually a convention of many academic essays. In other words, they are typical things that authors will use in genres like research papers, editorials, and even books. They are less common in narratives and profiles, even though those genres still have main ideas.

For your analysis essay, you will probably need a thesis for your paper. Here's a quick two-step process for drafting a tentative thesis. Remember, it's hard to write a thesis until you do research. It's also OK for your thesis to change depending on what sort of information you uncover while you're writing.

Step One: Write the Question You Are Trying to Answer

Often your instructor (in English 101 and other courses) will give you a question, but even if they don't you should try to identify one. Here's a possible example for the analysis paper.

> How does this advertisement for the Humane Society try to persuade its audience to donate?

Once you have a question, you are halfway to having a thesis. Also note, just as your thesis can change, you may find that you need to change your question, too. It all depends on what you uncover through your research and writing.

Step Two: Write an Answer to Your Question Using the Same Language

Use the language from your question to write an answer, even if it's just a guess at this point.

> The advertisement for the Humane Society tries to persuade its audience to donate by evoking emotions like sympathy through images of starving or abused animals and by telling the audience how even small amounts of money can have lasting effects.

There you have it. You can always change what you've written, but having a clear thesis will help your audience see your main point, and it can even help you clarify what it is you're trying to say.

Myths and Facts about Thesis Statements

There are a lot of myths and facts about thesis statements. It's important to know the difference. Here are a few to discuss as a class.

Fact: Thesis statements include a topic and a comment on the topic.

Myth: Thesis statements can only be one sentence long.

Fact: The best thesis statements are debatable.

Myth: Thesis statements must present one claim supported by three ideas.

Fact: Thesis statements will often appear at the end of the first paragraph of an academic essay.

NOTES

Activity: Planning and Organizing the Rhetorical Analysis Essay

Even though you may choose another pattern of organization for your essay, it's helpful to begin with a basic plan as you gather your evidence and anticipate your audience's needs and questions. This working outline is adapted from *Easy Writer.*

I. **Introduction**

- *Summarize* your text as concisely as possible (try to do this in three lines or less if you can).

____

____

____

____

____

____

- Provide your *thesis statement* by the end of paragraph 1. Write it out here.

____

____

____

____

____

____

II. **Background.** What do readers need to know to understand this text and your thesis? List that information here and *note your sources.*

____

____

____

____

____

____

NOTES

III. **Lines of Argument**

- Reason #1. State the first point you want to prove about your text. What evidence can you provide from your text or your research?

- Reason #2. State your next point. What evidence can you provide?

- Reason #3 *and so on*. Continue to assert your points clearly and back them with evidence. Make sure that each point ties back to the thesis statement you established on page 1.

IV. **Conclusion.** As you bring your analysis to a conclusion, you have several strategies to consider. Here are some you may want to adopt: (1) Elaborate on implications of your thesis statement. (2) Make clear what you want readers to think. (3) Make a strong ethical or emotional appeal in a memorable way. (4) Evaluate the text's effectiveness for its audience. (5) Evaluate the text's effectiveness for yourself. (You are also welcome to create a concluding strategy of your own.)

NOTES

5

Workshop: Peer Review for the Rhetorical Analysis

Author: ______________________________

Title: ______________________________

Reader: ______________________________

INTRODUCTION (base your responses just on the first paragraph for this section)

What text is the essay about? ______________________________

____

____

____

What is the main idea of the essay? ______________________________

____

____

____

What could the author do to make that main idea even clearer? ______________________________

____

____

____

____

____

____

AUTHOR

Who does the writer credit as the author(s) of the text? ______________________________

Explain how the information given about the author relates or does not relate to the essay's main idea. What was going on in the author's life or in history that influenced the text?

____

____

____

____

____

Ask one question about the author that might help your understanding of the text.

AUDIENCE

Who does the author describe as the audience of this text? ____________________

Do you think this has changed over time? If so, explain how.

Were there any historically significant events that contributed to the text, its audience, and the interpretation? Describe how this works or does not work in the essay.

THE TEXT ITSELF

How frequently is the actual text referred to in a specific way?

Are there instances where rhetorical appeals are referenced to explain how the text works? Y/N

Make at least one suggestion to improve this section or describe one strength.

Finally, comment on the use of citations and works cited. Are they correct? How many sources are there? What types are they? How does this affect the author's *ethos*?

5 Reflective Cover Memo

Date: ______________________________

To (Instructor's Name): ______________________________

From (Author of Paper): ______________________________

Subject: ______________________________

Reflective Cover Memo for "Final for Now"—Rhetorical Analysis

Writing Process. Please reflect on your writing process. What did you try for the first time? What comments from peer workshop and conferences did you explore in your revision? How did this improve your paper? Please describe concrete examples.

____

____

____

____

____

____

Purpose. What is your thesis statement/argument? What evidence did you use to support your overall argument? List the major points of your analysis in skeleton form. Now, briefly reflect on how effectively you think you put this analysis together and communicated it.

____

____

____

____

____

____

Context. How did you discuss the author, audience, and the text itself? How was your analysis original? What unique things do you think you had to say about this text?

____

____

____

____

____

____

Future Writing. What plans do you have for revisions of this paper for the final portfolio draft?

Questions or Comments. What questions do you have for me about the construction of your paper or the writing process? What would you like me to focus on while I read the "Final for Now" version of this paper?

NOTES

POLISHING YOUR PAPER

Insufficient Citation

The third most common mistake among first-year writers is insufficient citation. This means that writers will make reference to a source but forget to include an in-text citation or all of the information that is necessary for a reader. Here is an example:

> Andrea Lunsford explains that "source citations demonstrate that you've done your homework on your topic and that you are a part of a conversation surrounding it."

While the sentence above clearly contains a direct quote, it does not provide enough information to the reader about where the quote came from. Instead, the sentence should look like this:

> Andrea Lunsford explains that "source citations demonstrate that you've done your homework on your topic and that you are a part of a conversation surrounding it" (208).

The second sentence tells the reader not only that the quote came from Andrea Lunsford but also that the reader can find the quote on page 208 of the book.

Here are two strategies for identifying places that need sufficient citation in your writing.

1. **Strategy #1: On the Computer**. Use the word processor's highlight or underline feature to mark all passages that reference outside sources. This will give you a visual signal for identifying all of the material that comes from someone else. It is especially helpful if you find yourself copying quotes from other electronic sources directly into your writing. Remember that insufficient citation is linked to plagiarism concerns. Be thoughtful and careful when copying text from other sources to support your arguments.

   Use section 41c of *Easy Writer* to help you craft in-text citations for each reference.

2. **Strategy #2: On Paper**. Write all of your quotes, paraphrases, and any other references to outside sources on 3 × 5 inch notecards and then tape or paste them onto a page of your writing wherever they will appear. This, too, will give you a visual signal for identifying all of the spots that come from your sources.

   Use section 41c of *Easy Writer* to help you craft in-text citations for each reference.

For more on using MLA documentation styles, see Chapter 41 in *Easy Writer*.

NOTES

SAMPLE ANALYSIS

Tori Hawkins Hawkins 1

Christina Seymour

English 101-035

15 March 2012

What Have You Discovered?

Have you ever written to get things off your mind no matter how it is said on the paper? Then when you reread it, it tends to sound like one of your best pieces yet, minus the few mistakes that can easily be repaired. This is where the best of many writers comes out by just allowing their hand to write as their brain tells them something worthwhile, allowing the bottled up thoughts to escape on paper. This is either how Diane Lockward could have written "My Husband Discovers Poetry" on the whim of just putting words on paper or she could have written it when she was really angry and meant it at one point. I find the last part hard to believe after finding out that this is her husband's most favorite poem written by her. Diane Lockward writes a spiteful yet comedic poem, portraying the lack of love that she made up about her spouse that captivates the audience by making them ponder on every stanza.

Author

To write about Lockward is hard when only a short brief paragraph that says the same thing on every website can be found. Lockward is a former high school teacher who has become a poet-in-the-schools for both the New Jersey State Council on the Arts and the Geraldine R. Dodge Foundation (Lockward). Diane is a native to New Jersey and has kept the decision to reside there. A decent biography on her is scarce to come across. Diane has received many rewards for her writings and presented to audiences in various ways. She was awarded the Quentin R. Howard Poetry Prize (Red). Her poems have appeared in journals like *Beloit Poetry Journal, Spoon*

NOTES

River Poetry Review, *Poetry International*, *Poet Lore*, and *Prairie Schooner* (Red). Also, Diane has received the 2003 Poetry Fellowship from the New Jersey State Council on the Arts (Red). So, the best information to go by is the brief summary that comes above the poem. This poem, when first read, can be interpreted a thousand ways. But once it is known that it is her husband's most favorite poem written by her, it inspires a bit of amusement in the reader's mind. Every relationship has its struggles. I believe Lockward wrote this poem as if her marriage did not have the typical affection that shows when the man and woman love each other.

Audience

Many types of audiences can be invigorated by this poem. It can be read by a woman who goes through a rough patch with her husband, a person who loves to read poetry, or someone whose spouse may have broken the relationship with a mistake that has been made. Even though not only women can have a calling to this poem some men in an abusive relationship, where the woman abuses him, could also possibly like this poem. No matter what the relationship status of the reader, this poem can be quirky to one, spiteful to another, or an inspiration to someone else:

> I wrote about a night years after we parted / when my husband's coldness drove me from the house / and back to my old boyfriend. / I even included the name of a seedy motel / well-known for hosting quickies, / I have a talent for verisimilitude. (Lockward)

The word that comes into mind while reading the part of stanza two is "adultery." Adultery means "voluntary sexual intercourse between a married person and another who is not his or her spouse, regarded as a violation of the marriage vows and hence as a sin or crime; the state or condition of having committed this" ("Adultery"). If someone going through a rough patch in a relationship feels as if that

NOTES

is what is going on with the spouse, the poem might show up on a search on the Internet. It can bring many of inspirations to the women who might not receive enough attention—maybe allowing them to create a quirky idea as to how to get their spouse or loved one to pay them the attention they are lacking. The poem could also give off a negative vibe. There might be the people out there who read this and take it to heart as to, "Oh, I could do this and cheat too without it being wrong" morals. This idea might be a little far-fetched, but it could happen.

Text

Striking words, chosen to create strong details and images, were picked very carefully to depict a strong message. One word, coldness, was used twice to describe the husband. This word as it is used in this poem is defined as being "marked by a lack of the warmth of normal human emotion, friendliness, or compassion" ("Coldness"). By using it twice to describe the husband makes this something of importance that Lockward wanted to tell her audience. By starting out with the first coldness, she can then bring it to the next portion of the story. This poem, like *The Canterbury Tales*, it is a "framed piece of art." The frame of this story uses many negative words to explain a reason why this woman would cheat on her husband. These next few lines are the end of the first stanza and the beginning of the second that are the part of the frame that touches the picture. It is telling one story while trailing off to begin another.

> In lines of strict iambic pentameter, / I detailed his coldness, his lack of humor. It felt good to do this. / Stanza by stanza, I grew bolder and bolder. / Towards the end, struck by inspiration. (Lockward)

Hawkins 4

NOTES

When it gets into the picture it is detailed to explain the connection that the writer has with this old boyfriend. Even though it is an old boyfriend, stated in the second stanza, the third stanza just mentions him as being "my boyfriend." This gives the feeling that even though she did not love him enough to marry him, she still had very strong feelings towards him up to that day. The woman records,

> In sensuous images, I described / how my boyfriend and I stripped off our clothes, / got into bed, and kissed and kissed, / then spent half of the night telling jokes, / many of them about my husband. / I left the ending deliberately ambiguous, / then hid the poem away / in an old trunk in the basement (Lockward).

It describes feelings that may not have been aroused in the woman for a while from her husband that "her boyfriend" was able to receive. This contrasts with the way that the husband treats her, giving the poem more depth and meaning in the end. Lockward created a spiteful atmosphere when she is sensually describing the encounter then leaving the ambiguous ending to draw out a suspicion of wonder that becomes comedic.

The final part of the frame mentions how after she is done writing it, she goes down to the basement and slips it into an old trunk. Then Lockward adds more conflict but only as conflict within the husband. "Do you see the wounded creature / at the bottom of the stairs, / his shoulder hunched over and shaking, / fist in his mouth and choking back sobs? / It was my husband paying tribute to my art," says the woman (Lockward). The man finally realizes the way his wife feels after all. Years of being ignored and lack of attention towards her comes as a toll to his emotions finally.

NOTES

Conclusion

By giving a lot of information and not using many words, each stanza can be broken down to having more meaning than what is really written. She did an excellent job in this poem to create different meanings for whoever reads this poem. One can look at it every day for a week and find a message different from the last. Still gaping at how she could come up with a message like this while knowing that this is her husband's most favorite poem. It almost makes it comedic at the end. In the sensuous way the poem is detailed, one would almost believe that she did cheat on him with an ex-boyfriend, but still today they are happily married. Whatever the process was taken to write this poem, many props goes to Diane. Lockward successfully captures the audience with her surprisingly witty poem, "My Husband Discovers Poetry."

NOTES

Hawkins 6

"Adultery." *The Oxford English Dictionary*. 3rd ed. 2012. *OED Online*. Oxford University Press. 23 April 2012.

"Coldness." Merriam-Webster. 2012.

Lockward, Diane. "My Husband Discovers Poetry." *Poetry, A Pocket Series*, edited by R.S. Gwynn. New York: Pearson, 2007. Print

Red Room Omnimedia Corporation. Wind Publications. 2012. 14 Mar. 2012.

NOTES

CHAPTER 6
Writing to Describe Perspectives

Chapter 6 is the last major project of the course prior to the portfolio. In this unit, we'll analyze an issue by researching the different people who have a stake in it. We'll also examine what it means to let your research guide your thesis.

GETTING STARTED

Overview of Project: Writing to Describe Perspectives

PURPOSE

You've probably heard the expression, "There's two sides to every story." The purpose of this assignment is to use what you've learned about telling stories, collecting information, and conducting analysis in order to explain not just two but multiple sides to a complex issue.

GENRE

The genre we're going to use for this chapter is the exploratory essay. In an exploratory essay, you start with a central question or tentative idea. Then you conduct research to learn more about that question or idea. Finally, you explain what you learned through your exploration.

AUDIENCE

Your instructor may have specific instructions about what audience to write for. Otherwise, consider writing for an audience of people invested in the issue you are discussing. Be mindful of how people with differing ideas would react to your writing. Don't just write for the people who agree with you. Try not to alienate the people who don't agree with you. Ask yourself, "How can I get the people who disagree on this issue to listen to what I'm saying?"

NOTES

ORGANIZATION

You've probably realized by now that there are almost always options for organizing a piece of writing. As a writer, you have to think critically about what information should come first, what should come second, and so on. You'll have to do that again here, but remember what you've learned about introductions, conclusions, works cited pages, and MLA format. In addition, because this paper asks you to explain multiple perspectives, you'll need to consider a range of people who have a stake in your issue (i.e., stakeholders) and find information that will help you explain their points of view.

ASSESSMENT

Your instructor may adjust the criteria below to fit the specific project for your course. In any case, here are a few key criteria to keep in mind:

- Focus on one meaningful issue
- Write a clear tentative thesis or research question at the beginning of your essay
- Find information that helps you explain multiple perspectives
- Integrate sources effectively with appropriate citations
- Organize your argument in a way that makes a difficult issue easy to understand
- Use an engaging voice that draws in readers with diverse points of view
- Produce approximately 1,500 to 1,750 words (5–6 pages) of polished writing

In many cases, the choice of topic for this unit is up to you, although your instructor may have a theme to help you focus your ideas.

One way to get started on a project is to complete a freewrite about a topic of interest to you. Take a look at the three topics listed below:

- Blogging
- Free College Tuition
- Food on Campus

Just for practice, pick one of these topics and complete a freewrite on it. Remember, a freewrite is a short, timed writing exercise. You should not stop writing, and you should not worry about grammar or punctuation. Just get your ideas onto the page.

Try it now. For the next 2 minutes, write down everything you know, think you know, or want to know about one of these topics. Do it right here in the book.

On your mark. Get set. Go!

NOTES

NOTES

Activity: Creating a Plan for the Exploratory Essay

Date: ______________________________

To: ______________________________

From: ______________________________

Subject: A Working Plan for the Exploratory Essay

Please fill in the sections below to give me a clear sense of your working plan for this paper.

Research Question. What issue have you selected? Try to phrase a key question or two that your project will address.

____

____

____

____

____

____

Research Plans. What articles, books, or other texts have you found, or when do you plan to do some library research? Whom might you interview, survey, or ask for input? Have you made sure that your research represents more than one perspective on the issue?

____

____

____

____

____

____

Purpose. What is the focus of the whole project? What is the purpose? How are you sure that you have a focus that is specific enough to allow you to say something unique, without wasting time on generalities?

____

____

____

____

____

____

DOES THIS PAPER HAVE A THESIS?

NOTES

Since we talked about thesis statements in the last chapter, we want to address them again here because exploratory essays may ask you to do something different than what you're used to.

Recall that a thesis is a statement that clearly explains an author's main idea for a piece of writing (Lunsford 371) and that thesis statements are conventions of many academic essays.

For your exploratory essay, you want to focus on allowing your thesis to develop as you research different perspectives and stakeholders. In other words, you shouldn't pick a position on an issue and then try to prove it. That's the typical approach.

Instead, you want to start with a **working thesis** that describes what you think the answer is. Then as you explore the issue by doing research on different perspectives and stakeholders, you may find your thesis growing, changing, and developing. That's a good thing.

For this reason, your instructor *may* ask you to put your working thesis or research question in the introduction and then your revised (or final) thesis at the conclusion in order to mark the end of your exploration of the issue. In other words, you still have a thesis, it's just located in a different place because you're writing in a different genre.

On the other hand, your instructor may still ask you to place your thesis at the end of the first paragraph of your essay. Then, the rest of your paper will support and explain that thesis.

Either way is fine. Just listen to your instructor and remember: You can't really write your thesis until you do your research.

NOTES

Activity: Audience and the Exploratory Essay

Now that you have a topic and a research question and have had time to do a little research, how will you frame a thesis to reach an audience that includes more than one stakeholder (including some readers who may disagree with your view)? What rhetorical claims and appeals might you make to your audience? Where will you start? How will you anticipate questions or opposition? Where will you integrate research to provide support for your argument?

If your topic is, for instance, wind power, here's how you might begin:

1. You've narrowed the topic to look at the issue locally: wind power and its effect on West Virginians.
2. Who are some stakeholders? Politicians, local residents, environmental activists, and state tourism advocates.
3. Once you have identified several stakeholders, think about what perspective each represents. For example, would state tourism advocates see the issue in economic terms? Be sure that you have chosen stakeholders who represent a broad range of perspectives on the issue.
4. Which stakeholders will be your primary readers? Who else might you persuade? What evidence will you need to support your position? For instance, if you want to persuade politicians to support wind power, how might you argue for cleaner energy options using emissions data? Are there economic advantages you might also cite? What opposition might you anticipate?
5. Think about the stance you want to take, the readers you want to persuade, the ways you'll use your research to make your case, and the type of rhetorical strategies and appeals that might be useful. Fill out the chart on the next page to help you organize your ideas.

	WHY IS THEIR PERSPECTIVE INTERESTING AND IMPORTANT?	WHAT RESEARCH DO YOU NEED TO DO TO UNDERSTAND AND ACKNOWLEDGE THEIR PERSPECTIVE?	WHAT RHETORICAL STRATEGIES MIGHT APPEAL TO THIS READER—AND WHY?
STAKEHOLDER 1			
STAKEHOLDER 2			
STAKEHOLDER 3			
STAKEHOLDER 4			

NOTES

USING WVU LIBRARIES ONLINE

What are LibGuides? LibGuides are websites created by WVU librarians to help students and researchers find course- or topic-specific resources in one place. For instance, you can find WVU LibGuides on folklore, African American history, interior design, psychology, and much more.

How can the English 101 LibGuide help you? The English 101 LibGuide offers a single place from which you can do all of your research. You can get ideas about potential topics; use Library databases to find journal, magazine, and newspaper articles; search the Libraries' online catalog for books; and even chat online with a librarian if you need help.

Use the 101 LibGuide to find topics for any of your papers using CQ Researcher. Find relevant newspaper or magazine coverage of an issue for your Feature Article using the LexisNexis search. Find scholarly articles for your rhetorical analysis or exploratory essays using Academic Search Premier. Use a LexisNexis search to find news articles from a specific date to help you learn about historical context for your narrative or rhetorical analysis essay. The 101 LibGuide not only gathers these resources in one place, but the site also shows you how to best use these resources. If you ever get stuck, check out the tutorials or actually contact a librarian via chat or e-mail.

How do you get there? The WVU LibGuides' home is located at *http://libguides.wvu.edu*.

- At the WVU LibGuides' homepage, find the left-hand menu, **Browse by Subjects**. As you can see, we have LibGuides for many different subjects.
- Choose **English**. You'll then be taken to a page with all of the LibGuides for English.
- Click on the link **English 101 Research Guide** (*http://libguides.wvu.edu/english101*).

Resources are arranged by sections: **Home**, for information about Library services; **Find a Research Question**, for exploring possible essay topics; **Find Journal and Newspaper Articles**, for popular sources; **Find Peer Reviewed Articles**, for scholarly articles; **Web Search** for using the Web effectively and evaluating Web resources; **Getting Help**, for chatting, e-mailing, or consulting with a librarian.

NOTES

USING CQ RESEARCHER

For this project, it is important to find a topic and then narrow this topic down so that you can create a manageable and unique research question. Then, you also need to do research to better understand who the stakeholders are for your issue. Finally, you need to find research to explore the positions of each of your stakeholders. CQ Researcher is a great place to start this work.

The WVU English 101 Research LibGuide is located at *http://libguides.wvu.edu/english101.*

- From the 101 LibGuide page, click on the tab labeled **One-Stop Research**.
- Then click on the link that says **CQ Researcher**.

Searching CQ Researcher

There are two ways that you can search CQ Researcher: either by **Browse Topic** (best if you have a broad topic that you want to research and need to narrow it down) and **Quick Search** (best if you have a narrow topic and keywords already).

BROWSE TOPIC

- Check out the demo video. It will show you how to use the **Browse Topic** link to find good, focused research questions and walk you through a report's features.
- Look at the recent reports on CQ Researcher or look through the list of topics and try to find a topic that interests you. Then, when you browse the report for this topic, you can begin to narrow your topic down and create your own research question.

QUICK SEARCH

- If you have a focused research question already, list your keywords and use the **Quick Search** box to find reports.

Using a CQ Researcher Report

CQ Reports all have the following sections: Introduction; Overview; "The Issues" Subheadings; Background; Current Situation; Outlook; Pro/Con; Chronology; Short Features; Footnotes/Bibliography; Contacts; About the Author; Document Citation.

Let's examine the CQ report *Middle Class Squeeze: Is More Government Aid Needed?* (6 March 2009) to see how you can use a report to find a research question, determine stakeholders, and do some added research. [Go to *CQ Researcher* on Libraries' Databases page (*http://www.libraries.wvu.edu/databases/*) to see this report; CQ is listed under C.]

NOTES

The **Subheadings** on the issues surrounding the topic often make good focused research questions and let you know who is affected by a particular issue—who the stakeholders are. The sections *Is a stable middle class a thing of the past?; Is overconsumption at the root of the middle class' problems?; Are aggressive new government programs needed to bolster the middle class?* all would make excellent focused research questions. Further, these questions identify stakeholders: legislators, members of the middle class, people who market to middle-class consumers, banks who loan to the middle class, employers of middle class workers, and so on.

The **Short Features** section usually discusses side issues to the topic at hand and can offer more potential research questions. For example, both *What Does 'Middle Class' Really Mean?* and *Economic Meltdown Batters Retirement Plans: Reform proposals call for limiting risk to workers* would make good focuses for research papers and allow you to see more stakeholders in an issue, including people who expect to retire in the next few years, the recently unemployed, investment bankers, and so on.

The **Pro/Con** section presents two essays, each arguing one side of an issue. The Pro/Con essay for *Middle Class Squeeze* asks *Has U.S. trade and globalization policy hurt the middle class?* This would make yet another focused way to examine the broader issue of middle-class economic woes. Those arguing the two sides can be seen as stakeholders themselves and as authorities on these issues. Remember, a good paper will examine the many sides of an issue.

Don't forget to use the **Bibliography** and **Footnotes** section to get started on research; many of the sources are linked to online full-text articles.

NOTES

HOW TO USE THE POINTS OF VIEW REFERENCE CENTER DATABASE

Points of View is a free database made available to students at WVU through the library's website. This is a great database to use for your exploratory essay as it gathers a variety of opinions and perspectives on issues.

The easiest way to get to this database is to log on to the WVU English 101 Research LibGuide (libguides.wvu.edu/english101).

Step 1: Click on the One-Step Research tab.

Step 2: Click on Points of View Reference Center.

This is the homepage of the database:

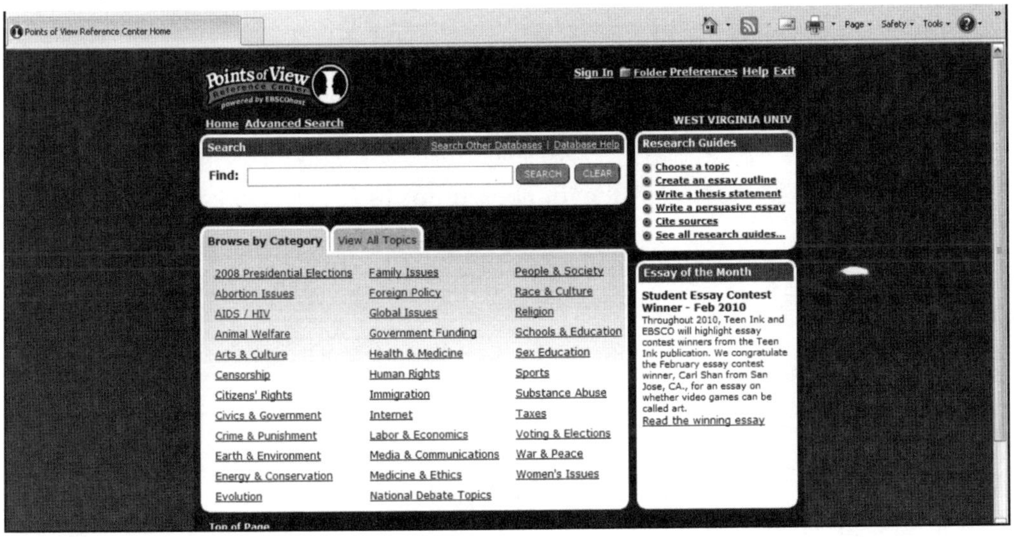

1. **Research Shelf** (located in the upper right-hand corner of the homepage) offers advice on how to write your paper.

NOTES

2. **Search** allows people who have a topic in mind to input their own topics of interest and locate corresponding articles and images. What makes this database unique is that it sorts its findings under a number of tabs (All Results, Points of View, Periodicals, Newspapers, etc.). The default is "Points of View," so you will want to check out the other tabs or click on "All Results" to see the rest of the available resources. (For example, a quick search for "Strip Mining" returns four "Points of View" articles.)

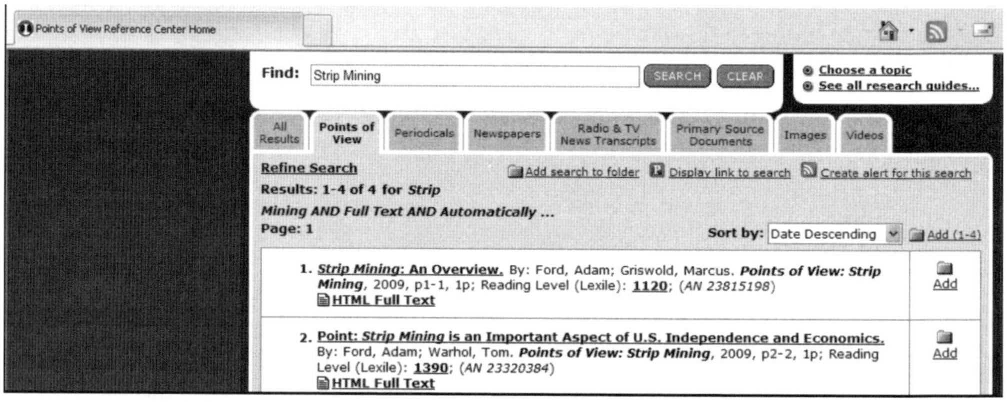

When you click on "Periodicals," the number jumps to 72 search results.

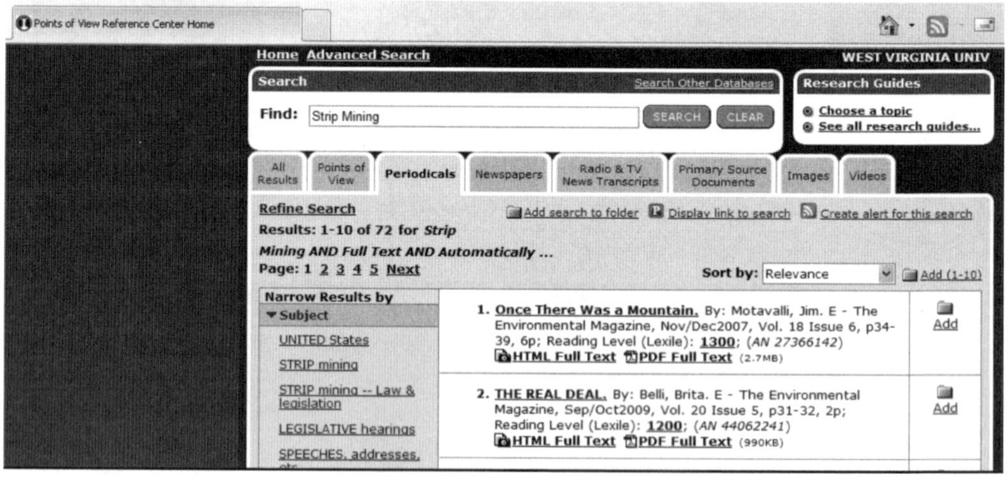

("All Results" yields a total of 505 search results.)

Advanced Search Options allows you to limit your search by document type and publication date. This also allows you to search only for PDF Full Text articles and Peer Reviewed articles. This may be useful depending on your requirements for the papers.

NOTES

When you find articles you are interested in, you can add them to a folder for easy retrieval later, download them, or print them off. If you like a particular article, you can click on the link "Find More Like This" at the top of the index page, and it will take you to similar articles.

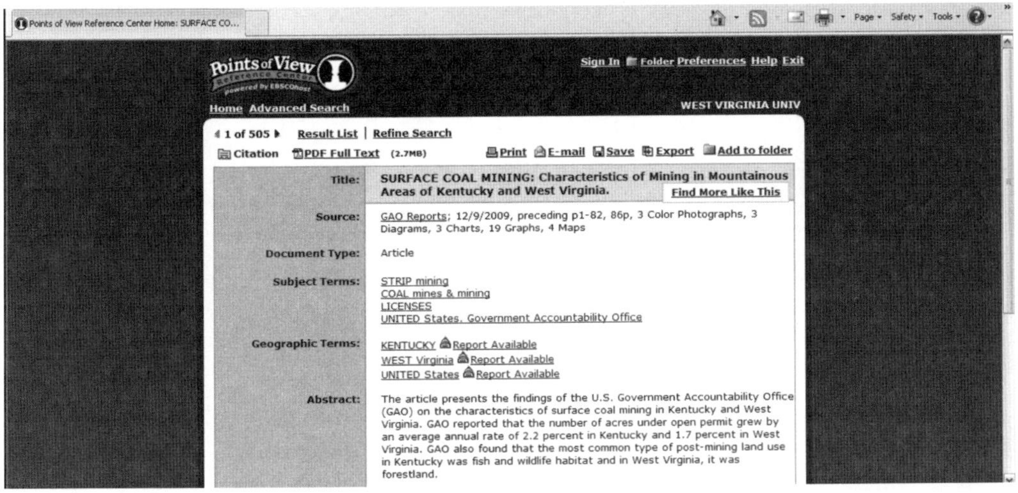

NOTES

6 Reflective Cover Memo

Date: ____________________

To (Instructor's Name): ____________________

From (Author of Paper): ____________________

Subject: ____________________

Reflective Cover Memo for "Final for Now"—Exploratory Essay

Writing Process. Please reflect on your writing process. What worked? What did you try for the first time? Did you take any risks? What are you most proud of? Anything you found challenging? What else should I know about how this paper evolved?

Changes and Revisions. What changed between your initial research question and the "Final for Now" version? Why?

Analyzing Your Own Writing. Perform a very brief rhetorical analysis of your own paper. What are the dominant rhetorical strategies and appeals that you used to make your argument persuasive to your audience?

Future Writing. What else might you have discussed in this paper if you had more time/space? What plans do you have for revisions of this paper for the final portfolio?

Questions or Comments. Is there anything you'd like me to keep in mind as I read the "Final for Now" version of this paper?

6 Workshop: Peer Review for the Exploratory Essay

Author:____

Title: ____

Reader:____

Writers: What type of response would be most useful to you at this stage in your writing?

Readers: As you read, please write down your answers to the questions the writer has identified. As usual, go ahead and write directly on the draft you're reading, and *please remember to sign your comments*.

1. Please read the draft through once for an **INITIAL RESPONSE**.
   - What was your **first impression** of the paper as a whole?
   - What **reaction** did it leave you with?
2. Please read through the paper for **FOCUS AND AUDIENCE**.
   - What is the **main idea and focus** of the draft? Please mark the place in the paper where the main idea comes across.
   - Does the main idea need to be clarified or focused further? Does the main idea need to be introduced sooner?
   - Who seems to be the **audience** for this paper? How can you tell? What might help reach the intended audience? Can you suggest an alternative audience?
3. Please read the paper to look at **EVIDENCE AND DOCUMENTATION.**
   - Where does the writer offer **evidence** beyond his/her own experience?
   - How does the writer introduce the evidence?
   - When passages or examples are cited, does the writer explain how and why they're significant? Do the examples continually relate back to the main idea?
   - Are sources fully acknowledged? Check the in-text citations and Works Cited for accuracy.
   - Identify at least one place where you need more evidence or more explanation.
4. Please read the paper to look at **ORGANIZATION**.
   - How does the writer group information and signal transitions to help the essay cohere?
   - Try a sentence outline, OR a list of possible section headings, OR a traditional outline, OR a flowchart to look at the organization. Suggest one way the writer might develop the topic.
   - Suggest anything else that would improve the organization or development of the paper.

Activity: Reverse Outlining to Check Organization

One common strategy of organization is called **reverse outlining**. The "reverse" here indicates that this tactic is used after you've written an initial draft, or at least most of one. You then create an outline of what you've written. This lets you (or a reader) take a step back from the draft to evaluate the strengths and weaknesses of the organization and the argument itself.

1. **Reread the Draft Carefully.**

   Read your paper over, and as you do so, identify the thesis, and then make very brief notes in the margin about what each paragraph is trying to say and do. Essentially, you are meant to be tracking the ideas in your paper as they collectively build toward a persuasive argument (which is ideally captured in your thesis statement).

2. **Outline the Draft.**

   After you've read through the entire essay, transfer the brief notes into a list in the order they appear in the essay. The goal is to say not only *what* each paragraph says but also *how* it advances the argument.

   Para 1 tries to *(Introduce the topic? Capture the reader's attention? Both? How?)*

   ____

   Para 2 tries to ______________________________

   Para 3 ______________________________________

   Para 4 ______________________________________

   Para 5 ______________________________________

   Para 6 ______________________________________

   Para 7 ______________________________________

   Para 8 ______________________________________

   Para 9 ______________________________________

   Para 10 _____________________________________

   Para 11 _____________________________________

   Para 12 _____________________________________

   And so on (using the reverse side or another piece of paper if needed).

3. **Examine the Thesis, the Outline, and the Draft Together.**

   Look closely at the outline and see how it holds up as a model for demonstrating the validity of the thesis statement. You should be able to determine which paragraphs need to be better connected, if they are in a logical order, and if any are irrelevant to the focus of your argument.

NOTES

POLISHING YOUR PAPER

Pronoun References

The fourth most common mistake among first-year writers has to do with pronoun references. This means that writers will use pronouns like *they* but do not clarify what exactly *they* refers to. Here is an example:

The cup of coffee on the table spilled onto the computer after it wobbled.

It's not clear in the sentence above what actually did the wobbling. Was it the cup, the table, or the computer? Editing the sentence can help make sure the audience doesn't get confused.

The cup of coffee on the table spilled onto the computer after the table wobbled.

Here are two strategies for identifying places that need clear pronoun references in your writing.

Strategy #1: On the Computer. Use the search feature in your word processor to search for pronouns like *her, his, it,* and *their*. Read each example one by one and decide whether the pronoun has a clear antecedent—the noun or noun phrase that a pronoun replaces.

Strategy #2: On Paper. Scan your paper for pronouns like *her, his, it,* and *their.* When you find one, highlight it. When you finish scanning for each, read each example one by one and decide whether the pronoun has a clear antecedent—the noun or noun phrase that a pronoun replaces.

For more on using pronouns, see chapter 11 in *Easy Writer*.

NOTES

SAMPLE EXPLORATORY ESSAY

Christianne Connelly
Ashleigh Petts
ENGL 101 Sec 038
April 12, 2012

More Pay for the Price

"I stand ready to deploy, engage, and destroy the enemies of the United States of America in close combat. I am a guardian of freedom and the American way of life. I am an American Soldier." What do these words mean to you? To a soldier it is a mix of words instilled in their hearts, a complex way of life, and the knowledge that the job is one of the most dangerous in the world. Taken from the end of the "Soldier's Creed," this excerpt reminds Americans that the life of a soldier is not always easy. From the tremendous amount of hours that our military works throughout the year to the dangerous risks involved when serving at home and across the seas, one cannot help but wonder if these men and women that are trained to protect the freedom of the United States are paid fairly, equally, and enough. Many civilians and Congressmen believe American soldiers do not need more tax money going into their pockets, but I believe military wages should be increased. Soldiers work extraneous hours, at times they do not have the privilege of seeing their families every day (whether it be because of training, deployment, or long hours at work), and their job is very exhausting both physically and mentally because of what has to be endured while deployed in to a warzone.

Currently, military pay is divided into several ranks based on the soldier's occupation. These ranks include E-1 to E-9, W-1 to W-5, and O-1 to O-10. Rank E stands for enlisted (without previous instruction) and is one of the lowest paid ranks in all of the military, but specifically, those E-4 and below are the least paid. E-4's and under make less than $23,000 a year according to the proposed 2012 base salary

NOTES

increase ("2012 Military Pay Scale Chart Table"). Ranks E-1 to E-4 automatically change. After six months E-1 soldiers move to E-2, then a year later they become an E-3, and after two years of service soldiers become an E-4. Those ranked E-5 to E-9 have reached non-commissioned officer status which is harder to change in terms of ranks (Samples). E-9 soldiers make $58,000 a year, but that is only obtained after ten years of service. W, meaning warrant officer, makes approximately $33,000 a year and after twenty years of service they can make up to $83,000 at their highest rank, W-5. Officers, O, begin their salary at $42,000 and at their highest rank, O-10, will make about $188,000 after twenty years of service ("2012 Military Pay Chart Scale").

Opposing Arguments

President Barrack Obama has recommended a 1.6 percent increase for those in the military for the 2012 budget (O'Keefe). But is that enough? Last year the lowest ranks, E-1–E-4, made at or below $22,900 before taxes and with the increase, these ranks will make $23,300 which is still much lower than the working class average salary (Powers).

Also the Pentagon announced in January that the U.S. should limit pay raises to troops, increase health insurance fees for retired soldiers, and close bases to save money on the new budget for 2012 (Bumiller and Shanker). Defense Secretary, Leon E. Panetta, also mentioned the Army would decrease in size from 570,000 to 490,000 troops in five years and the Marines would be lowered to 182,000 troops from 202,000 (Bumiller and Shanker). In relation to how the U.S. military is supposed to fulfill all of its duties with such drawbacks, both Mr. Panetta and Gen. Martin E. Dempsey, the chairman of the Joint Chiefs of Staff, said that the United States military would still remain the best in the world. General Dempsey said, "Capability is more important than size" (Bumiller and Shanker).

NOTES

Those in power are not the only ones opposing an increase for military salaries. There are also citizens that believe soldiers are paid well over enough while they are deployed, but they may not be aware of the smaller details. Combat pay includes the soldiers' base salary and an added $225 a month plus a family separation allowance of $250 a month if the soldier is married, which is tax free (Powers). If the soldiers are single and live on base, they must pay to keep their belongings in storage because while they are gone, their barracks will be used for other soldiers and the deployed soldiers will have a new place to live upon returning from deployment. Also, there is money deducted from soldiers' salary while they are deployed and it is used to pay for the MREs (meal ready to eat) to have food in order to survive (Samples).

But what about times when there is not a war for soldiers to be deployed to? Soldiers will not receive that bonus pay and will have to survive solely on base pay to take care of their bills. It may also seem as if soldiers come home with plenty of money, but citizens must remember soldiers have this money because they have not been able to spend it as they were in a war zone for months, up to years at one time.

Supporting Research

While there is much hesitation to increase military salaries with the serious debt crisis in the United States, citizens and politicians must remember how disturbing the job of a soldier can be. The length of hours being worked and the lack of time spent with their families also come in to account. Soldiers living on base, participating in training, or being active in a war zone are on the clock 24/7.

While on base in the Army, a typical work day commences at about 5:50 A.M. Soldiers start the day with physical training for a few hours and then are able to take a short, almost one hour, break to change into uniforms and clean up from heavy perspiration created during complex fitness exercises. When promptly back to work,

Connelly 4

NOTES

the hours will vary. Depending on the tasks for each day soldiers may not be released until sometimes 8:00 in the evening, which is well over a twelve-hour work day. Although occasionally there are times soldiers are able to return home early in the afternoon if there is no other work to be completed (Samples).

The typical civilian occupation allows a set amount of time for a lunch break, but sometimes with a hectic work schedule in the Army, there is no time to eat lunch and soldiers must go on with their day. Also, if soldiers maintain a residence provided by the base, they may be called out for duty at any time to handle necessary tasks (Samples). With extended hours such as these, why should our country's soldiers have to settle for a fixed salary?

Although there are many hours here at home, across seas is a different story. Separated from their family and thousands of miles away from everything America's servicemen have ever known, soldiers do not have the chance to get off from work and relax, let alone talk to their families every day. Many times it is unknown when those deployed will talk to their loved ones again. As they continue to protect our country for several months at a time, soldiers risk their own lives and bodies within the dangers of warfare. The seriousness of the matter deserves more recognition from the U.S. government's funds especially for those ranked below an officer's status of E-4 and under.

Along with the worry of their families back home, soldiers also have to encounter many other detrimental scenes from the activity of warfare. Physically soldiers are worn down by heat, sand, lack of hygiene and sleep, always being alert, looking for hidden improvised explosive devices (IEDS), searching for targets and executing them, and also from pursuing missions during the day and night. After

NOTES

taking in consideration all of these, American citizens must remember soldiers are still human. The images they will see are unbearable and for what the United States Army, Marines, Navy, and Air Force get paid, it becomes a question of if it is really worth the risk. These soldiers could make the same amount of money at home, safely, without having to deal with the exhausting stressfulness and harsh activity seen during war.

U.S. soldiers may witness many horrifying entities and thus could cause endangerment to the soldier's mental health for when they arrive home. Watching comrades die, helping fallen soldiers and civilians in the war site, taking out targets, coming across people with bombs, not knowing who to trust, these are all examples of what soldiers go through within a warzone. Seeing vicious and cruel images while overseas will harm soldiers mentally because those images will never be erased and for some they will be replayed over and over again. Soldiers today are more susceptible than ever to developing Post Traumatic Stress Disorder (PTSD) after coming home (Samples).

Personal Stake

Prior to 2011, I never understood much about the military. I did not know of the rules and the regulations, or of the particulars. I just went about my life like any other normal teenager. My then boyfriend Tyler, who is now my fiancé, left for basic training in April 2011. His MOS (military occupation specialty or job) in the military is infantry and over the course of those four months, I really obtained a lot of insight from the training he had to go through. I was only able to communicate with him through letters and occasionally a phone call that would only last for about fifteen minutes or less which was very rare. Although it was not until he was stationed in Washington State that I really took this issue into consideration.

NOTES

Connelly 6

I knew Tyler was not paid a lot, I understood that, but as he would tell me more and more about his job and what he had to do, I felt the need to do something about it. I bring this issue to light because, not only Tyler, but every hardworking soldier deserves more money for their occupation. They are constantly working and I hardly even get to see my fiancé. Unlike civilians, soldiers do not have the choice to take off work whenever they feel like it because that decision is up to the company commander. Each day soldiers are up before 5:00 A.M. in order to arrive on time to work, and most often they have to stay late hours. With their salary, in some cases, bills consume all of the money from one paycheck, and there is none left to buy food. Sure there is a place for single soldiers to eat on base, but it is often closed by the time Tyler and his co-workers get off work. Money is drawn out of their paycheck for the cafeteria food they are supposed to be able to eat every month, but is often wasted because of its early closing hours and their long working hours.

Training here in the United States is also risky. In November my fiancé was involved in an accident during training in which one man died and many others were injured. I can only imagine what could possibly happen during his time in the actual war. In a few weeks Tyler will be deploying to Afghanistan. We are not married yet, so when he comes home in nine months, he still will not have very much money. Also, Tyler has had extensive training from going to sniper school, which was supposed to provide a large bonus if completed, but even after finishing number one out of everyone, the bonus was only a mere twenty-five dollars more a month. His job is very difficult and he is not the only soldier that deserves more money for what he does for a living. I have definitely become more educated through his experiences, and I hope the United States government and its citizens can recognize the urgency and unfairness of this issue.

NOTES

The life of a soldier is not easy in any way. After deep concentration on what American soldiers go through, whether it is from the mental and physical toughness of their job to months up to years of separation from their families, military servicemen and women are owed much higher wages than what they currently receive. Soldiers like Tyler are what protect this nation from its enemies. Military men and women know they will make a small yearly salary, and yet they still seek to sign up even with loved ones left at home. Imagine yourself in my shoes: your significant other is going off to war and risking his or her life in multiple dangerous situations on a daily basis. But what for? A low living? And in the meantime, all you can do is sit and wait for a chance to hear from him/her while you pray to God they are doing okay. At times I feel it is not worth the risk, but my fiancé does it because it is his job and so others do not have to. For all of the extensive training, long days of work, separation from loved ones, and health risks involved with this kind of occupation, these soldiers deserve a higher-paying salary. It is important that Americans support the troops because without soldiers risking their own lives every day and sacrificing time spent with their family, our nation would not be what it is today. Being in the military is not like an average day job and as a result, my hope is that American citizens will recognize the severity of this matter in order for it to one day be changed, so every soldier will get paid what they deserve.

Connelly 8

NOTES

Works Cited

"2012 Military Pay Scale Chart Table." *Military Factory*. Military Factory,1 Jan. 2012. Web. 4 April 2012.

Bumiller, Elisabeth and Shanker, Thom. "Defense Budget Cuts Would Limit Raises and Close Bases." *New York Post*. New York Post, 26 Jan. 2012. Web. 29 Mar. 2012.

O'Keefe, Ed. "Budget 2012: Civilian and Military Pay Increases." *The Washington Post*. The Washington Post, 14 Feb. 2011.Web. 29 Mar. 2012.

Powers, Rod. "Current Military Pay Charts." *About.com*. About.com, 17 Oct. 2011. Web. 29 Mar. 2012.

Samples, Tyler. Personal Interview. 30 Mar. 2012.

NOTES

CHAPTER 7

Writing to Show What You Know

GETTING STARTED

Overview of Project: Writing to Show What You Know

PURPOSE

This is it. The last project. The purpose of this project is to reflect on everything you've learned so far this term AND demonstrate what you've learned to your instructor. How well you do at this task will determine the biggest portion of your grade for the course. It's time to focus, work, and show what you know.

GENRE

The genre that we're going to use for this project is the portfolio. A portfolio is a collection of work that demonstrates a person's skills and abilities. In this context, your final portfolio should consist of a reflective introduction, at least one draft of each major project, all of your polished formal writing projects (which should total about 20 or more pages of writing), and possibly a selection of writing you did in class or for homework. Your instructor will clarify any other elements that should or should not be included.

AUDIENCE

Your audience for this project is your instructor. It's often helpful to think of your whole portfolio as a persuasive text. Your thesis is that you are a better writer than you were when you began this class. You'll need to use all you've learned about rhetoric, writing, description, finding information, and analyzing to show your instructor just how much you've mastered.

ORGANIZATION

For this assignment, think critically about how best to organize your portfolio. Collect feedback on your organization from peers and your instructor. Make choices.

NOTES

ASSESSMENT

As at the midterm, all English 101 courses have the same core criteria for assessing portfolios. There are two places in this book that you can look for portfolio assessment criteria. The first is on the back inside cover of this book. This is really more of a checklist to help you think about and reflect on the course goals. The second place is the rubric on page 2 that describes what superior portfolios look like, what strong portfolios look like, what satisfactory portfolios look like, and so on.

TURNING IT IN

The assignment is due: ________________

I need to ____

____

____

FREEWRITE

NOTES

Remember freewriting is an activity meant to help you come up with ideas and record them. Recall, too, that there are two rules for freewriting aimed at helping you get the most out of the activity:

1. **Do not worry about spelling, grammar, and punctuation.**
2. **Do not stop writing.**

In order to start shaping your portfolio, take 3 minutes right now to do a freewrite on rhetoric. In other words, write down everything you know about rhetoric—all the ideas, terms, applications, strategies, questions, you name it—as quickly as you can. Ready. Set. Go!

Great work! You've already started shaping the reflective introduction to your portfolio. Much of what you've written here can be valuable information for that document. Try repeating this activity for the other course goals.

NOTES

MAKING A REVISION PLAN

At the end of the semester, students often have a lot of work to do and not much time to do it. Therefore, it helps to be thoughtful about how you're spending your time. Instead of working your way through all of your projects in the order you did them, use this form to help you identify where you need to spend the most time and what you can accomplish most quickly.

Project #1: Narrative

My final-for-now draft was at the brainstorming/discussion/professional stage.

I've spent __________ hours on this project since I turned in my final-for-now draft.

If I had two more days to work on this project, I would need to . . .

____

____

____

____

____

Project #2: Profile

My final-for-now draft was at the brainstorming/discussion/professional stage.

I've spent __________ hours on this project since I turned in my final-for-now draft.

If I had two more days to work on this project, I would need to . . .

____

____

____

____

____

Project #3: Rhetorical Analysis

My final-for-now draft was at the brainstorming/discussion/professional stage.

I've spent __________ hours on this project since I turned in my final-for-now draft.

If I had two more days to work on this project, I would need to . . .

____

____

____

____

____

Project #4: Exploratory Essay

NOTES

My final-for-now draft was at the brainstorming/discussion/professional stage.

I've spent __________ hours on this project since I turned in my final-for-now draft.

If I had two more days to work on this project, I would need to . . .

____

____

____

____

____

Now that you've thought about each project, you need to choose a strategy for revision that works for you. Will you start with the one that needs the most work so that you can be certain you have time to make significant improvements? Will you start with the one that needs the least amount of work so that you can finish it quickly and focus on other ones? You'll need to decide for yourself based on your available time, work load, and energy level.

And remember, sometimes it can help to discuss your plan with someone. Try reviewing your plan with your instructor, a friend, or a consultant in the Eberly Writing Studio.

NOTES

ADDITIONAL READING

Bird by Bird: Some Instructions on Writing and Life

ANNE LAMOTT

The first useful concept is the idea of short assignments. Often when you sit down to write, what you have in mind is an autobiographical novel about your childhood, or a play about the immigrant experience, or a history of—oh, say—women. But this is like trying to scale a glacier. It's hard to get your footing, and your fingertips get all red and frozen and torn up. Then your mental illnesses arrive at the desk like your sickest, most secretive relatives. And they pull up chairs in a semicircle around the computer, and they try to be quiet but you know they are there with their weird coppery breath, leering at you behind your back.

What I do at this point, as the panic mounts and the jungle drums begin beating and I realize that the well has run dry and that my future is behind me and I'm going to have to get a job only I'm completely unemployable, is to stop. First I try to breathe, because I'm either sitting there panting like a lapdog or I'm unintentionally making slow asthmatic death rattles. So I just sit there for a minute, breathing slowly, quietly. I let my mind wander. After a moment I may notice that I'm trying to decide whether or not I am too old for orthodontia and whether right now would be a good time to make a few calls, and then I start to think about learning to use makeup and how maybe I could find some boyfriend who is not a total and complete fixer-upper and then my life would be totally great and I'd be happy all the time, and then I think about all the people I should have called back before I sat down to work, and how

NOTES

I should probably at least check in with my agent and tell him this great idea I have and see if *he* thinks it's a good idea, and see if he thinks I need orthodontia—if that is what he is actually thinking whenever we have lunch together. Then I think about someone I'm really annoyed with, or some financial problem that is driving me crazy, and decide that I must resolve this before I get down to today's work. So I become a dog with a chew toy, worrying it for a while, wrestling it to the ground, flinging it over my shoulder, chasing it, licking it, chewing it, flinging it back over my shoulder. I stop just short of actually barking. But all of this only takes somewhere between one and two minutes, so I haven't actually wasted that much time. Still, it leaves me winded. I go back to trying to breathe, slowly and calmly, and I finally notice the one-inch picture frame that I put on my desk to remind me of short assignments.

It reminds me that all I have to do is to write down as much as I can see through a one-inch picture frame. This is all I have to bite off for the time being. All I am going to do right now, for example, is write that one paragraph that sets the story in my hometown, in the late fifties, when the trains were still running. I am going to paint a picture of it, in words, on my word processor. Or all I am going to do is to describe the main character the very first time we meet her, when she first walks out the front door and onto the porch. I am not even going to describe the expression on her face when she first notices the blind dog sitting behind the wheel of her car—just what I can see through the one-inch picture frame, just one paragraph describing this woman, in the town where I grew up, the first time we encounter her.

E. L. Doctorow once said that "writing a novel is like driving a car at night. You can see only as far as your headlights, but you can make the whole trip that way." You don't have to see where you're going, you don't have to see your destination or everything you will pass along the way. You just have to see two or three feet ahead of you. This is right up there with the best advice about writing, or life, I have ever heard.

NOTES

So after I've completely exhausted myself thinking about the people I most resent in the world, and my more arresting financial problems, and, of course, the orthodontia, I remember to pick up the one-inch picture frame and to figure out a one-inch piece of my story to tell, one small scene, one memory, one exchange. I also remember a story that I know I've told elsewhere but that over and over helps me to get a grip: thirty years ago my older brother, who was ten years old at the time, was trying to get a report on birds written that he'd had three months to write, which was due the next day. We were out at our family cabin in Bolinas, and he was at the kitchen table close to tears, surrounded by binder paper and pencils and unopened books on birds, immobilized by the hugeness of the task ahead. Then my father sat down beside him, put his arm around my brother's shoulder, and said, "Bird by bird, buddy. Just take it bird by bird."

I tell this story again because it usually makes a dent in the tremendous sense of being overwhelmed that my students experience. Sometimes it actually gives them hope, and hope, as Chesterton said, is the power of being cheerful in circumstances that we know to be desperate. Writing can be a pretty desperate endeavor, because it is about some of our deepest needs: our need to be visible, to be heard, our need to make sense of our lives, to wake up and grow and belong. It is no wonder if we sometimes tend to take ourselves perhaps a bit too seriously. So here is another story I tell often.

In the Bill Murray movie *Stripes*, in which he joins the army, there is a scene that takes place the first night of boot camp, where Murray's platoon is assembled in the barracks. They are supposed to be getting to know their sergeant, played by Warren Oates, and one another. So each man takes a few moments to say a few things about who he is and where he is from. Finally it is the turn of this incredibly intense guy named Francis. "My name is Francis," he says. "No one calls me Francis—

anyone here calls me Francis and I'll kill them. And another thing. I don't like to be touched. Anyone here ever tries to touch me, I'll kill them," at which point Warren Oates jumps in and says, "Hey—lighten up, Francis."

This is not a bad line to have taped to the wall of your office. Say to yourself in the kindest possible way, Look, honey, all we're going to do for now is to write a description of the river at sunrise, or the young child swimming in the pool at the club, or the first time the man sees the woman he will marry. That is all we are going to do for now. We are just going to take this bird by bird. But we are going to finish this one short assignment.

SHITTY FIRST DRAFTS

Now, practically even better news than that of short assignments is the idea of shitty first drafts. All good writers write them. This is how they end up with good second drafts and terrific third drafts. People tend to look at successful writers, writers who are getting their books published and maybe even doing well financially, and think that they sit down at their desks every morning feeling like a million dollars, feeling great about who they are and how much talent they have and what a great story they have to tell; that they take in a few deep breaths, push back their sleeves, roll their necks a few times to get all the cricks out, and dive in, typing fully formed passages as fast as a court reporter. But this is just the fantasy of the uninitiated. I know some very great writers, writers you love, who write beautifully and have made a great deal of money, and not *one* of them sits down routinely feeling wildly enthusiastic and confident. Not one of them writes elegant first drafts. All right, one of them does, but we do not like her very much. We do not think that she has a rich inner life or that God likes her or can even stand her. (Although when I mentioned this to my priest friend Tom, he said you can safely assume you've created God in your own image when it turns out that God hates all the same people you do.)

NOTES

Very few writers really know what they are doing until they've done it. Nor do they go about their business feeling dewy and thrilled. They do not type a few stiff warm-up sentences and then find themselves bounding along like huskies across the snow. One writer I know tells me that he sits down every morning and says to himself nicely, "It's not like you don't have a choice, because you do—you can either type or kill yourself." We all often feel like we are pulling teeth, even those writers whose prose ends up being the most natural and fluid. The right words and sentences just do not come pouring out like ticker tape most of the time. Now, Muriel Spark is said to have felt that she was taking dictation from God every morning—sitting there, one supposes, plugged into a Dictaphone typing away, humming. But this is a very hostile and aggressive position. One might hope for bad things to rain down on a person like this.

For me and most of the other writers I know, writing is not rapturous. In fact, the only way I can get anything written at all is to write really, really shitty first drafts.

The first draft is the child's draft, where you let it all pour out and then let it romp all over the place, knowing that no one is going to see it and that you can shape it later. You just let this childlike part of you channel whatever voices and visions come through and onto the page. If one of the characters wants to say, "Well, so what, Mr. Poopy Pants?," you let her. No one is going to see it. If the kid wants to get into really sentimental, weepy, emotional territory, you let him. Just get it all down on paper, because there may be something great in those six crazy pages that you would never have gotten to by more rational, grown-up means. There may be something in the very last line of the very last paragraph on page six that you just love, that is so beautiful or wild that you now know what you're supposed to be writing about, more or less, or in what direction you might go—but there was no way to get to this without first getting through the first five and a half pages.

I used to write food reviews for *California* magazine before it folded. (My writing food reviews had nothing to do with the magazine folding, although every single review did cause a couple of canceled subscriptions. Some readers took umbrage at my comparing mounds of vegetable puree with various ex-presidents' brains.) These reviews always took two days to write. First I'd go to a restaurant several times with a few opinionated articulate friends in tow. I'd sit there writing down everything anyone said that was at all interesting or funny. Then on the following Monday I'd sit down at my desk with my notes, and try to write the review. Even after I'd been doing this for years, panic would set in. I'd try to write a lead, but instead I'd write a couple of dreadful sentences, XX them out, try again, XX everything out, and then feel despair and worry settle on my chest like an x-ray apron. It's over, I'd think, calmly. I'm not going to be able to get the magic to work this time. I'm ruined. I'm through. I'm toast. Maybe, I'd think, I can get my old job back as a clerk-typist. But probably not. I'd get up and study my teeth in the mirror for a while. Then I'd stop, remember to breathe, make a few phone calls, hit the kitchen and chow down. Eventually I'd go back and sit down at my desk, and sigh for the next ten minutes. Finally I would pick up my one-inch picture frame, stare into it as if for the answer, and every time the answer would come: all I had to do was to write a really shitty first draft of, say, the opening paragraph. And no one was going to see it.

So I'd start writing without reining myself in. It was almost just typing, just making my fingers move. And the writing would be *terrible*. I'd write a lead paragraph that was a whole page, even though the entire review could only be three pages long, and then I'd start writing up descriptions of the food, one dish at a time, bird by bird, and the critics would be sitting on my shoulders, commenting like

NOTES

cartoon characters. They'd be pretending to snore, or rolling their eyes at my overwrought descriptions, no matter how hard I tried to tone those descriptions down, no matter how conscious I was of what a friend said to me gently in my early days of restaurant reviewing. "Annie," she said, "it is just a piece of *chicken*. It is just a bit of *cake*."

But because by then I had been writing for so long, I would eventually let myself trust the process—sort of, more or less. I'd write a first draft that was maybe twice as long as it should be, with a self-indulgent and boring beginning, stupefying descriptions of the meal, lots of quotes from my black-humored friends that made them sound more like the Manson girls than food lovers, and no ending to speak of. The whole thing would be so long and incoherent and hideous that for the rest of the day I'd obsess about getting creamed by a car before I could write a decent second draft. I'd worry that people would read what I'd written and believe that the accident had really been a suicide, that I had panicked because my talent was waning and my mind was shot.

The next day, though, I'd sit down, go through it all with a colored pen, take out everything I possibly could, find a new lead somewhere on the second page, figure out a kicky place to end it, and then write a second draft. It always turned out fine, sometimes even funny and weird and helpful. I'd go over it one more time and mail it in.

Then, a month later, when it was time for another review, the whole process would start again, complete with the fears that people would find my first draft before I could rewrite it.

Almost all good writing begins with terrible first efforts. You need to start somewhere. Start by getting something—anything—down on paper. A friend of mine says that the first draft is the down draft—you just get it down. The second draft is

NOTES

the up draft—you fix it up. You try to say what you have to say more accurately. And the third draft is the dental draft, where you check every tooth, to see if it's loose or cramped or decayed, or even, God help us, healthy.

What I've learned to do when I sit down to work on a shitty first draft is to quiet the voices in my head. First there's the vinegar-lipped Reader Lady, who says primly, "Well, *that's* not very interesting, is it?" And there's the emaciated German male who writes these Orwellian memos detailing your thought crimes. And there are your parents, agonizing over your lack of loyalty and discretion; and there's William Burroughs, dozing off or shooting up because he finds you as bold and articulate as a houseplant; and so on. And there are also the dogs: let's not forget the dogs, the dogs in their pen who will surely hurtle and snarl their way out if you ever stop writing, because writing is, for some of us, the latch that keeps the door of the pen closed, keeps those crazy ravenous dogs contained.

Quieting these voices is at least half the battle I fight daily. But this is better than it used to be. It used to be 87 percent. Left to its own devices, my mind spends much of its time having conversations with people who aren't there. I walk along defending myself to people, or exchanging repartee with them, or rationalizing my behavior, or seducing them with gossip, or pretending I'm on their TV talk show or whatever.

I speed or run an aging yellow light or don't come to a full stop, and one nanosecond later am explaining to imaginary cops exactly why I had to do what I did, or insisting that I did not in fact do it.

I happened to mention this to a hypnotist I saw many years ago, and he looked at me very nicely. At first I thought he was feeling around on the floor for the silent alarm button, but then he gave me the following exercise, which I still use to this day.

NOTES

Close your eyes and get quiet for a minute, until the chatter starts up. Then isolate one of the voices and imagine the person speaking as a mouse. Pick it up by the tail and drop it into a mason jar. Then isolate another voice, pick it up by the tail, drop it in the jar. And so on. Drop in any high-maintenance parental units, drop in any contractors, lawyers, colleagues, children, anyone who is whining in your head. Then put the lid on, and watch all these mouse people clawing at the glass, jabbering away, trying to make you feel like shit because you won't do what they want—won't give them more money, won't be more successful, won't see them more often. Then imagine that there is a volume-control button on the bottle. Turn it all the way up for a minute, and listen to the stream of angry, neglected, guilt-mongering voices. Then turn it all the way down and watch the frantic mice lunge at the glass, trying to get to you. Leave it down, and get back to your shitty first draft.

A writer friend of mine suggests opening the jar and shooting them all in the head. But I think he's a little angry, and I'm sure nothing like this would ever occur to you.

SOMEONE TO READ YOUR DRAFTS

There's an old *New Yorker* cartoon of two men sitting on a couch at a busy cocktail party, having a quiet talk. One man has a beard and looks like a writer. The other seems like a normal person. The writer type is saying to the other, "We're still pretty far apart. I'm looking for a six-figure advance, and they're refusing to read the manuscript."

Now, I've been wrong before, but I'd bet you anything that this guy never shows his work to other writers before trying to get someone to buy it. I bet he thinks he's above that.

NOTES

Whenever I'm giving a lecture at a writing conference and happen to mention the benefits of finding someone to read your drafts, at least one older established writer comes up to me and says that he or she would never in a million years show his or her work to another person before it was done. It is not a good idea, and I must stop telling my students that it will help them. I just smile, geishalike, and make little fluttery sounds of understanding. Then I go on telling people to consider finding someone who would not mind reading their drafts and marking them up with useful suggestions. The person may not have an answer to what is missing or annoying about the piece, but writing is so often about making mistakes and feeling lost. There are probably a number of ways to tell your story right, and someone else may be able to tell you whether or not you've found one of these ways.

I'm not suggesting that you and another writer sit in a cubby somewhere and write together, as though you were doing potato prints side by side at the institution, and that then you beam at each other's work the way you gape when your kid first writes his name. But I am suggesting that there may be someone out there in the world—maybe a spouse, maybe a close friend—who will read your finished drafts and give you an honest critique, let you know what does and doesn't work, give you some suggestions on things you might take out or things on which you need to collaborate, ways in which to make your piece stronger.

In the first story of Donald Barthelme's I ever read, twenty years ago, he said that truth is a hard apple to catch and it is a hard apple to throw. I know what a painful feeling it is when you've been working on something forever and it feels done, and you give your story to someone you hope will validate this and that person tells you it still needs more work. You have to, at this point, question your assessment of this person's character and, if he or she is not a spouse or a lifelong friend, decide

NOTES

whether or not you want them in your life at all. Mostly I think an appropriate first reaction is to think that you don't. But in a little while it may strike you as a small miracle that you have someone in your life, whose taste you admire (after all, this person loves you and your work), who will tell you the truth and help you stay on the straight and narrow or find your way back to it if you are lost.

I always show my work to one of two people before sending a copy to my editor or agent. I feel more secure and connected this way, and these two people get a lot of good work out of me. They are like midwives; there are these stories and ideas and visions and memories and plots inside me, and only I can give birth to them. Theoretically I could do it alone, but it makes it easier to have people helping. I have girlfriends who've had their babies through natural childbirth—no drugs, no spinal, no nothing—and they secretly think they had a more honest birth experience, but I think the epidural is right up there with the most important breakthroughs in the West, like the Salk polio vaccine and salad bars in supermarkets. It's an individual thing. What works for me may not work for you. But feedback from someone I'm close to gives me confidence, or at least it gives me time to improve. Imagine that you are getting ready for a party and there is a person at your house who can check you out and assure you that you look wonderful or, conversely, that you actually do look a little tiny tiny tiny bit heavier than usual in this one particular dress or suit or that red makes you look just a bit like you have sarcoptic mange. Of course you are disappointed for a moment, but then you are grateful that you are still in the privacy of your own home and there is time to change.

One of the best writers I know has a wife who reads everything he writes and tells him when she loves it and when she doesn't, why it does or doesn't work for her. She is almost like an equal partner in the process. Two other writers I know use each other. As I said, I have two people who read my stuff. One is another writer, who is one of my best friends and probably the most neurotic, mentally ill person in my galaxy. Another is a librarian who reads two or three books a week but has never written a word. What I do is to work over a piece until it feels just about right, and then I send it to one of these two friends, who have agreed in advance to read it.

I always send my work Federal Express, because I am too impatient to wait for the mail to deliver it. I spend the entire next day waiting to hear, pacing, overeating, feeling paranoid and badly treated if I haven't heard from my friends by noon. Naturally I assume that they think it is tripe but that they don't have the courage to tell me. Then I'll think about all the things I don't like about either of them, how much in fact I hate them both, how it is no wonder that neither of them has many friends. And then the phone will ring and they usually say something along the lines of "I think it's going to be great, I think it's really good work. But I also think there are a few problems."

At this point, I am usually open to suggestion, because I am so relieved that they think it's going to be great. And I ask gaily where they think there's room for improvement. This is where things can get ever so slightly dicey. They might say that the whole first half is slow, and they couldn't get into it, but that on page six or thirty-eight or whatever, things finally got going, and then they couldn't put it down. They absolutely raced through the rest of it—except that maybe they had a bit of trouble with the ending, and they wonder if I really understand one character's motivation and whether I might just want to spend—oh—five minutes, no more, rethinking this person.

My first response if they have a lot of suggestions is never profound relief that I have someone in my life who will be honest with me and help me do the very best work of which I am capable. No, my first thought is, "Well. I'm sorry, but I can't be friends with you anymore, because you have too many problems. And you have a bad personality. And a bad character."

NOTES

NOTES

Sometimes I can't get words to come out of my mouth because I am so disappointed as if they had said that Sam is ugly and boring and spoiled and I should let him go. Criticism is very hard to take. But then whichever friend is savaging my work will suggest that we go through it together page by page, line by line, and in a clipped, high-pitched voice I'll often suggest that this won't be necessary, that everything's just fine. But these friends usually talk me into going through the manuscript with them over the phone, and if I'll hang in there, they'll have found a number of places where things could be so much stronger, or funnier, or more real, or more interesting, or less tedious. They may even have ideas on how to fix those places, and so, by the end, I am breathing a great sigh of relief and even gratitude.

When someone reliable gives you this kind of feedback, you now have some true sense of your work's effect on people, and you may now know how to approach your final draft. If you are getting ready to send your work to a potential agent for the first time, you don't want to risk burning that bridge by sending something that's just not ready.

You really must get your piece or book just right, as right as you can. Sometimes it is just a matter of fine-tuning, or maybe one whole character needs to be rethought. Sometimes the friend will love the feel of the writing, the raw material, and yet feel that it is a million miles from being done. This can be deeply disappointing, but again, better that your spouse or friend tell you this than an agent or an editor.

I heard Marianne Williamson say once, that when you ask God into your life, you think he or she is going to come into your psychic house, look around, and see that you just need a new floor or better furniture and that everything needs just a little cleaning—and so you go along for the first six months thinking how nice life is now that God is there. Then you look out the window one day and see there's a wrecking ball outside. It turns out that God actually thinks your whole foundation is shot and

NOTES

that you're going to have to start over from scratch. This is exactly what it can be like to give, say, a novel to someone else to read. This person can love it and still find it a total mess, in need of a great deal of work, of even a new foundation.

So how do I find one of these partners? my students ask. The same way you find a number of people for a writing group. The only difference is that in this case, you're looking for one partner instead of several. So if you are in a class, look around, see if there's someone whose work you've admired, who seems to be at about the same level as you. Then you can ask him or her if he or she wants to meet for a cup of coffee and see if you can work with each other. It's like asking for a date, so while you are doing this, you will probably be rolfed by all your most heinous memories of seventh and eighth grade. If the person says no, it's good to wait until you get inside your car before you fall apart completely. Then you cart rend your clothes and keen and do a primal scream. Of course, you probably want to be sure that the person hasn't followed you out to your car. But it actually doesn't matter if he or she sees you break down, because you don't have to be friendly with that person anymore. That person is a jerk. You double up therapy sessions for a few weeks until you're back in the saddle, and then you ask someone else; someone you like much better.

If you know for sure that some smart and civilized person loves your work, you can ask that person if she would be willing to look at a part of your novel or your latest short story. If this person writes, too, ask if she would like you to take a look at her draft. If she says no to both offers, pretend to be friendly, so she won't think less of you than she already does. Then you can move into a trailer park near your therapist's home until you're well enough again to ask someone else.

The second question my students ask about a writing partner is this: what if someone agrees to read and work on your stuff for you, and you have agreed to do the same for him, say, and it turns out that he says things about your work, even in the

NOTES

nicest possible tone of voice, that are totally negative and destructive? You find yourself devastated, betrayed. Here you've done this incredibly gutsy thing, shown someone your very heart and soul, and he doesn't think it's any good. He says how sorry he is that this is how he feels. Well, let me tell you this—I don't think he is. I think destroying your work gave him real pleasure, pleasure he would never cop to, pleasure that is almost sexual in nature. I think you should get rid of this person immediately, even if you are married to him. No one should talk to you like this. If you write a long piece, and it is your first, and you are wondering if it's publishable, and it isn't, even by a long shot, someone should be able to tell you this in a way that is gentle yet not patronizing, so that you are encouraged—maybe not to pursue publication, but to pursue writing. Certainly this person might suggest you get a second opinion. But if he is too strident or adamant, ditch the sucker. Would you stand for someone talking this way to your children—for instance, telling them that they are not very talented at painting and shouldn't even bother? Or that their poetry is not very interesting? Of course not. You'd want to go pay this person a little visit with your flame thrower. So why, if someone says something like this to you, would you want anything further to do with him? Why waste what little time you may have left with such scum?

I worry that Jesus drinks himself to sleep when he hears me talk like this. But about a month before my friend Pammy died, she said something that may have permanently changed me.

We had gone shopping for a dress for me to wear that night to a nightclub with the man I was seeing at the time. Pammy was in a wheelchair, wearing her Queen Mum wig, the *Easy Rider* look in her eyes. I tried on a lavender minidress, which is not my usual style. I tend to wear big, baggy clothes. People used to tell me I dressed like John Goodman. Anyway, the dress fit perfectly, and I came out to model it for her. I stood there feeling very shy and self-conscious and pleased. Then I said,

"Do you think it makes my hips look too big?" and she said to me slowly, "Annie? I really don't think you have that kind of time."

And I don't think you have that kind of time either. I don't think you have time to waste not writing because you are afraid you won't be good enough at it, and I don't think you have time to waste on someone who does not respond to you with kindness and respect. You don't want to spend your time around people who make you hold your breath. You can't fill up when you're holding your breath. And writing is about filling up, filling up when you are empty, letting images and ideas and smells run down like water—just as writing is also about dealing with the emptiness. The emptiness destroys enough writers without the help of some friend or spouse.

There are always a couple of rank beginners in my classes, and they need people to read their drafts who will rise to the occasion with respect and encouragement. Beginners always try to fit their whole lives into ten pages, and they always write blatantly about themselves, even if they make the heroine of their piece a championship racehorse with an alcoholic mother who cries a lot. But beginners are learning to play, and they need encouragement to keep their hands moving across the page.

If you look around, I think you will find the person you need. Almost every writer I've ever known has been able to find someone who could be both a friend and a critic. You'll know when the person is right for you and when you are right for that person. It's not unlike finding a mate, where little by little you begin to feel that you've stepped into a shape that was waiting there all along.

NOTES

Responding—Really Responding—to Other Students' Writing

RICHARD STRAUB

Okay. You've got a student paper you have to read and make comments on for Thursday. It's not something you're looking forward to. But that's alright, you think. There isn't really all that much to it. Just keep it simple. Read it quickly and mark whatever you see. Say something about the introduction. Something about details and examples. Ideas you can say you like. Mark any typos and spelling errors. Make your comments brief. Abbreviate where possible: *awk, good intro, give ex, frag*. Try to imitate the teacher. Mark what he'd mark and sound like he'd sound. But be cool about it. Don't praise anything really, but no need to get harsh or cutthroat either. Get in and get out. You're okay, I'm okay. Everybody's happy. What's the problem?

This is, no doubt, a way of getting through the assignment. Satisfy the teacher and no surprises for the writer. It might just do the trick. But say you want to do a *good* job. Say you're willing to put in the time and effort—though time is tight and you know it's not going to be easy—and help the writer look back on the paper and revise it. And maybe in the process learn something more yourself about writing. What do you look for? How do you sound? How much do you take up? What exactly are you trying to accomplish? Here are some ideas.

HOW SHOULD YOU LOOK AT YOURSELF AS A RESPONDER?

Consider yourself a friendly reader. A test pilot. A roommate who's been asked to look over the paper and tell the writer what you think. Except you don't just take on the role of The Nice Roommate or The Ever-Faithful Friend and tell her what she

---

"Responding—Really Responding—to Other Students' Writing" by Richard Straub from *The Subject is Writing, 4th Edition: Essays by Teachers and Students* by Wendy Bishop and James Strickland, Editors.

NOTES

wants to hear. *This all looks good. I wouldn't change a thing. There are a couple places that I think he might not like, but I can see what you're doing there. I'd go with it. Good stuff.* You're supportive. You give her the benefit of the doubt and look to see the good in her writing. But friends don't let friends think their writing is the best thing since *The Great Gatsby* and they don't lead them to think that all is fine and well when it's not. Look to help this friend, this roommate writer—okay, this person in your class—to get a better piece of writing. Point to problems and areas for improvement but do it in a constructive way. See what you can do to push her to do even more than she's done and stretch herself as a writer.

WHAT ARE YOUR GOALS?

First, don't set out to seek and destroy all errors and problems in the writing. You're not an editor. You're not a teacher. You're not a cruise missile. And don't rewrite any parts of the paper. You're not the writer; you're a reader. One of many. The paper is not yours; it's the writer's. She writes. You read. She is in charge of what she does to her writing. That doesn't mean you can't make suggestions. It doesn't mean you can't offer a few sample rewrites here and there, as models. But make it clear they're samples, models. Not rewrites. Not edits. Not corrections. Be reluctant at first even to say what you would do if the paper were yours. It's not yours. Again: Writers write, readers read and show what they're understanding and maybe make suggestions. What to do instead: Look at your task as a simple one. You're there to play back to the writer how you read the paper: what you got from it; what you found interesting; where you were confused; where you wanted more. With this done, you can go on to point out problems, ask questions, offer advice, and wonder out loud with the writer about her ideas. Look to help her improve the writing or encourage her to work on some things as a writer.

NOTES

HOW DO YOU GET STARTED?

Before you up and start reading the paper, take a minute (alright, thirty seconds) to make a mental checklist about the circumstances of the writing, the context. You're not going to just read a text. You're going to read a text within a certain context, a set of circumstances that accompany the writing and that you bring to your reading. It's one kind of writing or another, designed for one audience and purpose or another. It's a rough draft or a final draft. The writer is trying to be serious or casual, straight or ironic. Ideally, you'll read the paper with an eye to the circumstances that it was written in and the situation it is looking to create. That means looking at the writing in terms of the assignment, the writer's particular interests and aims, the work you've been doing in class, and the stage of drafting.

- *The assignment:* What kind of writing does the assignment call (or allow) for? Is the paper supposed to be a personal essay? A report? An analysis? An argument? Consider how well the paper before you meets the demands of the kind of writing the writer is taking up.
- *The writer's interests and aims:* What does the writer want to accomplish? If she's writing a personal narrative, say, is she trying to simply recount a past experience? Is she trying to recount a past experience and at the same time amuse her readers? Is she trying to show a pleasant experience on the surface, yet suggest underneath that everything was not as pleasant as it seems? Hone in on the writer's particular aims in the writing.
- *The work of the class:* Try to tie your comments to the concepts and strategies you've been studying in class. If you've been doing a lot of work on using detail, be sure to point to places in the writing where the writer uses detail effectively or where she might provide richer detail. If you've been working on developing

NOTES

arguments through examples and sample cases, indicate where the writer might use such methods to strengthen her arguments. If you've been considering various ways to sharpen the style of your sentences, offer places where the writer can clarify her sentence structure or arrange a sentence for maximum impact. The best comments will ring familiar even as they lead the writer to try to do something she hasn't quite done before, or done in quite the same way. They'll be comforting and understandable even as they create some need to do more, a need to figure out some better way.

- *The stage of drafting:* Is it an early draft? A full but incomplete draft? A nearly final draft? Pay attention to the stage of drafting. Don't try to deal with everything all at once if it's a first, rough draft. Concentrate on the large picture: the paper's focus; the content; the writer's voice. Don't worry about errors and punctuation problems yet. There'll be time for them later. If it's closer to a full draft, go ahead and talk, in addition to the overall content, about arrangement, pacing, and sentence style. Wait till the final draft to give much attention to fine-tuning sentences and dealing in detail with proofreading. Remember: You're not an editor. Leave these sentence revisions and corrections for the writer. It's her paper. And she's going to learn best by detecting problems and making her own changes.

WHAT TO ADDRESS IN YOUR COMMENTS?

Try to focus your comments on a couple of areas of writing. Glance through the paper quickly first. Get an idea whether you'll deal mostly with the overall content and purpose of the writing, its shape and flow, or (if these are more or less in order) with local matters of paragraph structure, sentence style, and correctness. Don't try to cover everything that comes up or even all instances of a given problem. Address issues that are most important to address in this paper, at this time.

NOTES

WHERE TO PUT YOUR COMMENTS?

Some teachers like to have students write comments in the margins right next to the passage. Some like to have students write out their comments in an end note or in a separate letter to the writer. I like to recommend using both marginal comments and a note or letter at the end. The best of both worlds. Marginal comments allow you to give a quick moment-by-moment reading of the paper. They make it easy to give immediate and specific feedback. You still have to make sure you specify what you're talking about and what you have to say, but they save you some work telling the writer what you're addressing and allow you to focus your end note on things that are most important. Comments at the end allow you to provide some perspective on your response. This doesn't mean that you have to size up the paper and give it a thumbs up or a thumbs down. You can use the end comment to emphasize the key points of your response, explain and elaborate on issues you want to deal with more fully, and mention additional points that you don't want to address in detail. One thing to avoid: plastering comments allover the writing; in between and over the lines of the other person's writing—up, down, and across the page. Write in your space, and let the writer keep hers.

HOW TO SOUND?

Not like a teacher. Not like a judge. Not like an editor or critic or shotgun. (Wouldn't you want someone who was giving you comments not to sound like a teacher's red pen, a judge's ruling, an editor's impatience, a critic's wrath, a shotgun's blast?) Sound like you normally sound when you're speaking with a friend or acquaintance. Talk to the writer. You're not just marking up a text; you're responding to the writer. You're a reader, a helper, a colleague. Try to sound like someone who's a reader, who's helpful, and who's collegial. Supportive. And remember: Even when you're tough and demanding you can still be supportive.

NOTES

HOW MUCH TO COMMENT?

Don't be stingy. Write most of your comments out in full statements. Instead of writing two or three words, write seven or eight. Instead of making only one brief comment and moving on, say what you have to say and then go back over the statement and explain what you mean or why you said it or note other alternatives. Let the writer know again and again how you are understanding her paper, what you take her to be saying. And elaborate on your key comments. Explain your interpretations, problems, questions, and advice.

IS IT OKAY TO BE SHORT AND SWEET?

No. At least not most of the time. Get specific. Don't rely on general statements alone. How much have generic comments helped you as a writer? "Add detail." "Needs better structure." "Unclear." Try to let the writer know what exactly the problem is. Refer specifically to the writer's words and make them a part of your comments. "Add some detail on what it was like working at the beach." "I think we'll need to know more about your high school crowd before we can understand the way you've changed." "This sentence is not clear. Were you disappointed or were they disappointed?" This way the writer will see what you're talking about, and she'll have a better idea what to work on.

DO YOU PRAISE OR CRITICIZE OR WHAT?

Be always of two (or three) minds about your response to the paper. You like the paper, but it could use some more interesting detail. You found this statement interesting, but these ideas in the second paragraph are not so hot. It's an alright paper, but it could be outstanding if the writer said what was really bothering her. Always be ready to praise. But always look to point to places that are not working well or that are not yet working as well as they might. Always be ready to expect more from the writer.

NOTES

HOW TO PRESENT YOUR COMMENTS?

Don't steer away from being critical. Feel free—in fact, feel obliged—to tell the writer what you like and don't like, what is and is not working, and where you think it can be made to work better. But use some other strategies, too. Try to engage the writer in considering her choices and thinking about possible ways to improve the paper. Make it a goal to write two or three comments that look to summarize or paraphrase what the writer is saying. Instead of *telling* the reader what to do, *suggest* what she might do. Identify the questions that are raised for you as you reader:

- Play back your way of understanding the writing:

  This seems to be the real focus of the paper, the issue you seem most interested in.

  So you're saying that you really weren't interested in her romantically?

- Temper your criticisms:

  This sentence is a bit hard to follow.

  I'm not sure this paragraph is necessary.

- Offer advice:

  It might help to add an example here.

  Maybe save this sentence for the end of the paper.

- Ask questions, especially real questions:

  What else were you feeling at the time?

  What kind of friend? Would it help to say?

  Do you need this opening sentence?

  In what ways were you "a daddy's little girl"?

- Explain and follow up on your initial comments:

  You might present this episode first. This way we can see what you mean when you say that he was always too busy.

  How did you react? Did you cry or yell? Did you walk away?

  This makes her sound cold and calculating. Is that what you want?

NOTES

- Offer some praise, and then explain to the writer why the writing works:

  Good opening paragraph. You've got my attention.

  Good detail. It tells me a lot about the place.

  I like the descriptions you provide—for instance, about your grandmother cooking, at the bottom of page 1; about her house, in the middle of page 2; and about how she said her rosary at night: "quick but almost pleading, like crying without tears."

HOW MUCH CRITICISM? HOW MUCH PRAISE?

Challenge yourself to write as many praise comments as criticisms. When you praise, praise well. Think about it. Sincerity and specificity are everything when it comes to a compliment.

HOW MUCH SHOULD YOU BE INFLUENCED BY WHAT YOU KNOW ABOUT THE WRITER?

Consider the person behind the writer when you make your comments. If she's not done so well in class lately, maybe you can give her a pick-me-up in your comments. If she's shy and seems reluctant to go into the kind of personal detail the paper seems to need, encourage her. Make some suggestions or tell her what you would do. If she's confident and going on arrogant, see what you can do to challenge her with the ideas she presents in the paper. Look for other views she may not have thought about, and find ways to lead her to consider them. Always be ready to look at the text in terms of the writer behind the text.

Good comments, this listing shows, require a lot from a reader. But you don't have to make a checklist out of these suggestions and go through each one methodically as you read. It's amazing how they all start coming together when you look at your response as a way of talking with the writer seriously about the writing, recording how you experience the words on the page, and giving the writer something to think about for revision. The more you see examples of thoughtful commentary and the more you try to do it yourself, the more you'll get a feel for how it's done.

NOTES

Here's a set of student comments on a student paper. They were done in the last third of a course that focused on the personal essay and concentrated on helping students develop the content and thought of their writing. The class had been working on finding ways to develop and extend the key statements of their essays (by using short, representative details, full-blown examples, dialogue, and multiple perspectives) and getting more careful about selecting and shaping parts of their writing. The assignment called on students to write an essay or an autobiographical story where they looked to capture how they see (or have seen) something about one or both of their parents—some habits, attitudes, or traits their parents have taken on. They were encouraged to give shape to their ideas and experiences in ways that went beyond their previous understandings and try things they hadn't tried in their writing. More a personal narrative than an essay, Todd's paper looks to capture one distinct difference in the way his mother and father disciplined their children. It is a rough draft that will be taken through one or possibly two more revisions. Readers were asked to offer whatever feedback they could that might help the writer with the next stage of writing (Figure 7-1).

NOTES

Jeremy

Todd
ENG 1
Rick Straub
Assignment 8b

"Uh, oh"

When I called home from the police station I was praying that my father would answer the phone. He would listen to what I had to say and would react comely, logical, and in a manner that would keep my mother from screaming her head off. If my Mother was to answer the phone I would have to explain myself quickly in order to keep her from having a heart attack.

I like this paragraph. It immediately lets the reader relate to you and also produces a picture in the reader's mind

When I was eleven years old I hung out with a group of boys that were almost three years older than me. The five of us did all the things that young energetic kids did playing ball, riding bikes, and getting in to trouble. [Because they were older they worried less about getting in trouble and the consequences of there actions than I did.] *Good point, makes it more unlikely that you should be the one to get caught*

My friends and I would always come home from school, drop our backpacks off and head out in the neighborhood to find something to do. Our favorite thing to do was to find construction cites and steal wood to make tree forts in the woods or skateboard ramps. So one day, coming home from school, we noticed a couple new houses being built near our neighborhood. It was a prime cite for wood, nails, and anything else we could get our hands on. We discussed our plan on the bus and decided that we would all meet there after dropping our stuff off at home. [I remember being a little at hesitant first because it was close to my house but beyond the boundaries my parents had set for me. Of course I went because I didn't want to be the odd man out and have to put up with all the name calling.] I dropped my bag off and I headed to the construction cite.

what other things did you do to get into trouble? or is it irrelevant?

great passage really lets the reader know what you were thinking

I meet my friends there and we began to search the different houses for wood and what not. We all picked up a couple of things and were about to leave when one of my friends noticed a what looked to be a big tool shed off behind one of the houses. It looked promising so we decided that we should check it out. Two of the boys in the group said that they had all the wood they could carry and said they were going home. The rest of us headed down to the shed to take a look.

Once there we noticed that the shed had been broken in to previously. The lock on it had been busted on the hinges were bent. I opened the door to the shed and stepped inside to take a look around while my friends waited outside. It was dark inside but I could tell the place had been ransacked, there was nothing to take so I decided to leave. I heard my to friends say some thing so turned back around to site of them running away. I thought that they were playing a joke on me so I casually walked

was there a reason you were first or did it just happen that way

Figure 7-1

NOTES

out only to see a cop car parked near one of the houses under construction. As soon as I saw that cop car I took off but was stopped when a big hand pulled at that back of my shirt. I watched my friends run until they were out of cite and then I turned around.

The cop had me sit in the squad car while he asked me questions. He asked me if I knew those kids that ran off and I said "Nnnnnoooooooo". He asked me if I had broken in to that shed and I said "Nnnnnoooooo". The cop wrote down what I was saying all the while shaking his head. Then he told me that I wasn't being arrested but I would have to go down to the station to call parents and have them pick me up. Upon hearing that I nearly soiled my undershorts. "My God, I'm dead. My mom is going to kill me".

what else happened at the police station? How long were you there?

At the station the officer showed me the whole station, jail cells and everything. An obvious tactic to try and scare me, which worked. That plus the thought of my mom answering the phone and me trying to explain what happened nearly made me sick.

"Wwwwhhhaatttt! You're where?" She would say.

"The police station mom," uh oh, hear it comes.

"Ooooohhhh my God, my son is criminal," so loud I would have to pull the phone away from my ear.

maybe you could say more as to why you think your mom is like this

She had this uncanny ability to blow things out of proportion right from the start. She would assume the worse and then go from there. This was a classic example of why I could never go to her if I had any bad news. She would start screaming, get upset, and then go bitch at my father. My father is a pretty laid back but when ever my mother started yelling at him about me, he would get angry and come chew me out worse than if I had just gone to him in the first place.

If my father were to answer the phone he would respond with out raising his voice. He would examine the situation in a logical manner and make a decision form there.

"Uhhmmm(long pause). You're at the police station."

"Yeah dad, I didn't get arrested they just had me come down here so I had to tell you."

"Uhm, so you didn't get arrested(long pause). Well(long pause), I'll come pick you up and will talk about then".

I feel like I can relate to my father much better then I can to my mother. He has a cool and collective voice that can take command of any situation. I always feel like he understands me, like he knows what I'm thinking all the time. This comes in real handy when I get in trouble.

I like the way you use dialogue in this section to illustrate how each of your parents would react and then explain to the reader what each of them are like. It works well.

Did your Dad get into trouble as a kid so he knows what it's like? Explain why he reacts as he does.

would he punish you anyway or could you just get away with things

I called home. Sweet beading on my lip.

"Hello", my mom said. Oh geez, I'm dead.

"Mom can I talk to dad?"

"Why, what's wrong?"

"Oh, nothing, I just need talk to him," yes, this is going to work!

"Hold on," she said.

"Hello," my father said.

"Dad, I'm at the police station," I told him the whole story of what happened. He reacted exactly as I expect he would.

"Uhhmmm(long pause). You're at the police station...........

I really like the ending, it tells the reader what is going to happen without having to explain it step, by step. Good paper, I like the use of dialogue. Pehaps more on your understanding of why your parents react as they do.

Figure 7-1 *continued*

NOTES

This is a full and thoughtful set of comments. The responder, Jeremy, creates himself not as a teacher or critic but first of all as a reader, one who is intent on saying how he takes the writing and what he'd like to hear more about:

> Good point. Makes it more unlikely that you should be the one to get caught.
>
> Great passage. Really lets the reader know what you were thinking.
>
> Was there a reason you were first or did it just happen that way?
>
> Would he punish you anyway or could you just get away with things?

He makes twenty-two comments on the paper—seventeen statements in the margins and five more in the end note. The comments are written out in full statements, and they are detailed and specific. They make his response into a lively exchange with the writer, one person talking with another about what he's said. Well over half of the comments are follow-up comments that explain, illustrate, or qualify other responses.

The comments focus on the content and development of the writing, in line with the assignment, the stage of drafting, and the work of the course. They also view the writing rhetorically, in terms of how the text has certain effects on readers. Although there are over two dozen wording or sentence-level errors in the paper, he decides, wisely, to stick with the larger matters of writing. Yet even as he offers a pretty full set of comments he doesn't ever take control over the text. His comments are placed unobtrusively on the page, and he doesn't try to close things down or decide things for the writer. He offers praise, encouragement, and direction. What's more, he pushes the writer to do more than he has already done, to extend the boundaries of his examination. In keeping with the assignment and the larger goals of the course, he calls on Todd in several comments to explore the motivations and personalities behind his parents' different ways of disciplining:

> Maybe you could say more as to why you think your mom is like this.
>
> Did your dad get into trouble as a kid so he knows what it's like? Explain why he reacts as he does.

NOTES

He is careful, though, not to get presumptuous and make decisions for the writer. Instead, he offers options and points to possibilities:

> Perhaps more on your understanding of why your parents react as they do.
> What other things did you do to get into trouble? Or is it irrelevant?

From start to finish he takes on the task of reading and responding and leaves the work of writing and revising to Todd.

Jeremy's response is not in a class by itself. A set of comments to end all commentary on Todd's paper. He might have done well, for instance, to recognize how much this paper works because of the way Todd arranges the story. He could have done more to point to what's not working in the writing or what could be made to work better. He might have asked Todd for more details about his state of mind when he got caught by the policeman and while he was being held at the police station. He might have urged him more to make certain changes. He might even have said, if only in a brief warning, something about the number of errors across the writing. But this is moot and just. Different readers are always going to pick up on different things and respond in different ways, and no one reading or response is going to address everything that might well be addressed, in the way it might best be addressed. All responses are incomplete and provisional—one reader's way of reading and reacting to the text in front of him. And any number of other responses, presented in any number of different ways, might be as useful or maybe even more useful to Todd as he takes up his work with the writing.

All this notwithstanding, Jeremy's comments are solid. They are full. They are thoughtful. And they are respectful. They take the writing and the writer seriously and address the issues that are raised responsibly. His comments do what commentary on student writing should optimally do. They tum the writer back into his writing and lead him to reflect on his choices and aims, to consider and reconsider his intentions as a writer and the effects the words on the page will have on readers. They help him see what he can work on in revision and what he might deal with in his ongoing work as a writer.

NOTES

NOTES

NOTES

JON SCOTT NELSON FIRST-YEAR WRITING AWARD

Sponsored by the WVU Department of English

Student Name ______________________________

Local Address ______________________________

____

Phone Number (please provide number that is easiest to reach you at)

____

Class Rank ______________________________

Student ID # ______________________________

Title(s) of Entry/ies	Genre(s)
______________	______________
______________	______________
______________	______________
______________	______________

Instructor's Name ______________________________

Jon Scott Nelson Contest Guidelines

The Jon Scott Nelson Freshman Writing Award recognizes outstanding writing by English 101 students. All students enrolled in English 101 during the current academic year are eligible. Up to five prizes are awarded annually ($100 each). Please submit essays written in an English 101 class.

- Expository writing developed for your English 101 class only
- All submissions must have been written for classes *at WVU.*
- Students' names should be removed from the entries. Attach this entry form instead.
- No entries submitted after the March deadline (specific date to be announced in Spring) will be accepted.

For more information, e-mail Marsha.Bissett@mail.wvu.edu

NOTES

STUDENT COURSE SUMMARY SHEET

Instructor's Name: ______________________________

Semester: ______________________________

Section Number: ______________________________

Student's Name: ______________________________

Mid-Semester "In Progress" Grade: ______________________________

Attendance Record

Number of Classes Late: ______________________________

Number of Classes Missed: ______________________________

Number of Conferences Missed: ______________________________

Total Number of Absences: ______________________________

Grades

Participation Grade: ______________________________

Final Exploratory Writing Grade: ______________________________

Submission Portfolio Grade: ______________________________

Final Course Grade: ______________________________

Relevant Commentary:

WORKS CITED

NOTES

"Annotate." *Merriam-Webster.com*. Merriam-Webster, 2015. Web. 26 Mar. 2015.

Bunn, Mike. "How to Read Like a Writer." *Writing Spaces* 2 (2011): 71–86. *Writingspaces.org*. Web. 27 Mar. 2015.

Carroll, Laura Bolin. "Backpacks vs. Briefcases: Steps Toward Rhetorical Analysis." *Writing Spaces* 1 (2010): 45–58. *Writingspaces.org*. Web. 3 Nov. 2014.

Lunsford, Andrea A. *Easy Writer*. 5th ed. Boston: Bedford/St. Martin's, 2014. Print.

NOTES